The Seven Year Trap

Back Office Observations of the
Business of Law and the Path to
Partnership

Charles Gillis

For the Gillis family and a bright future at Gillis North.

CONTENTS

About the Author

Charles Gillis started his career in legal administration on the ground floor of a law firm while putting himself through college. His first law firm job was more than 25 years ago, working as a humble Court House Runner, back in the days before the internet in an era when legal pleadings had to be printed, photocopied, hand-delivered, and stamped at the court in triplicate. He quickly worked his way up the ranks and held management positions in legal boutiques, middle-market firms, and a major international law firm. He has held positions and managed projects in virtually every aspect of legal administration, encountering issues in dozens of offices around the world and in numerous practice areas. During his time in law firm management, he saw many careers flourish and others falter, spun into irrecoverable tailspins.

After more than a quarter century of law firm management he began his own recruiting and consulting firm called Northside Human Strategies, specializing in attorney and executive placements, and consulting. Charles has a BA from the University of Texas at Austin, an MBA from the University of Texas at Dallas, and a Graduate Finance certificate from Southern Methodist University.

Prelude:
The Point of this Book

The first seven years of your career in law will likely determine how you spend the following 35 years in your practice — or whether you'll even be employed as a lawyer in the future.

Reread the sentence above again. It's absolutely true. This book was written to help you better understand the business of private practice law in the United States. By knowing the business and your role in it, you can identify avoidable obstacles and maximize your career success. In private practice, the goal for most people is to eventually become an Equity Partner or owner of a firm. With that goal in mind, this book will give you a fundamental awareness of the critical issues to help you lay the right foundation at the early stages of your career. Indeed, the first take-away from this book is a very important fact — what you do early in your career will have a lasting impact on what comes later.

The legal industry has experienced unprecedented change in the last decade. Demand for legal services has been relatively flat for years. Clients have changed the way they buy and pay for services and law firms struggle to retain them in a hyper-competitive marketplace. Technology has created huge changes in the efficiency of law, reducing the time lawyers can charge to complete tasks. Projects which used to fill a lawyer's entire week can now be accomplished in mere hours. Each year there are more than 120,000 active law students supplying an endless wave of new workers into an industry where there are more job applicants than vacant positions. The hunt for the best legal talent is a constant challenge for growing firms.

It's a tough business, but there are many resources to help you. Regardless of your ultimate end goals, if you want to succeed you'll find the path much easier if you understand the intricacies of the business model. That seems like an obvious statement from the outside, but on the inside the understanding and appreciation of this point varies wildly. Like all other businesses, law firms exist to make a profit. If they fail to make a profit they eventually cease to exist.

This book is a rough field manual with realistic observations of the industry. There are many career books written by successful senior law firm Partners. These books often have editorial advisors who teach at law schools. While these books are often well written, I believe people need a bigger dose of the unvarnished truth before they dive into something as challenging as a career in private practice. Successful law Partners may have great stories about how they were promoted into partnership decades ago, but that advice might not be entirely pertinent to a new law grad today. While most law schools do a great job teaching the law, many shield students from the harsher realities of the profession and don't do enough to prepare grads for careers which are supposed to provide a lifetime of stable employment. The reality is that not all people will succeed in this profession. This book is written from a business and career management viewpoint. I will explore scenarios of victory and defeat. Think of this book as a map through the minefield.

I am not a lawyer, but I spent more than 25 years managing almost every aspect of the business of law firms. The advice in this book comes from the Business Director's viewpoint. You will find success in this industry if you are able to help your firm accomplish their financial and strategic goals. I know the goals, and the written and unwritten rules. I know what works and what doesn't. As a Director behind the scenes, Associates and Equity Partners often came to me when they wanted to know the real story.

As a lawyer your focus will be on the law, not business administration. Most successful law firms hire business people like me to run the operational aspects of their firm. When lawyers do anything other than practice the law or develop their practice, the firm is probably losing money. As a lawyer you don't want to spend time reconciling checkbooks, updating software, or writing job descriptions for a new help desk coordinator position. You want to practice the law. Professionals like me take care of your business, so you can focus on your highest purpose, which is serving your client's legal needs.

Over the years I've accumulated a great deal of wisdom which I present in this book. As a law firm business executive, much of my work was done outside the view of young lawyers. As a leader in firm management, I was part of the group that tracked and evaluated everything. If you were a lawyer at my firm I knew your productivity numbers. I wrote and managed the budgets you lived under. I was part of the discussions about your performance, prospects, and potential. I was at the table when the firm discussed starting salaries, raises, and bonuses. I was part of the promotion discussions. If you failed, I was the guy at your termination meeting, discussing key points of your severance package. Administrators like me work under the direction of the top lawyers in the firm. They carry institutional wisdom, often serving successive leadership changes above them. While the lawyers in law firm management may change over time, the dutiful admin team is often there for ages.

The industry is changing, and you need to arm yourself with as much information as possible. This information will help you progress in your career while avoiding many of the hidden traps that could delay or even end your journey. You need to understand what really matters at law firms and the important things which should happen at the different phases of your career. Not all of your future employers will be good at explaining these things.

For many years legal professionals felt above the ordinary din of commonplace business practices because they sincerely felt they were special, and in many ways, they were. It wasn't that long ago when most law firms even avoided advertising, because such actions were deemed beneath the profession. Years ago, there seemed to be more than enough work for lawyers and the number of law firms grew steadily. Fees charged to clients grew as well, as did the Partner's paychecks. While there were brilliant lawyers leading those firms, the rank and file lawyers at the junior level often lacked any real business experience or training outside of the legal industry. Many lawyers advanced through their careers without ever getting a strong grasp on law firm financial issues. Ask a lawyer if they can tell you what their firm's profit margin is and you're likely to hear some creative answers which may or may not be accurate.

This book assumes you are or want to be a lawyer, and a successful one. If you want to reach the top rung on the law ladder this is your book. Even if you aren't that ambitious, you'll still find helpful information here to support your goals. For some of you, reaching the pinnacle of private practice is not your top priority. You may simply wish to have a rewarding career practicing law, or you may be in the mix only for a regular paycheck. That's okay too. Regardless of what you want in your career, or whatever level of success you are hoping to achieve, your odds will be enhanced if you educate yourself on the business of law.

To be clear, this book concentrates on private practice law in the United States. While many of the issues discussed are applicable to legal practices in other jurisdictions, its primary focus is private practice in the U.S. This book is applicable to at least five different audiences:

1. Undergrad students considering future law studies

It is never too early to start thinking about a career in law. Many successful lawyers felt a calling for their chosen vocation early in life. Maybe you were inspired by legal dramas on television. Maybe you found inspiration by watching some of the leading jurists and legislators. Regardless of what it was that brought you here, if you are considering how to best position yourself for a future career in the law, you'll find ample resources in this book to help you greet the future prepared with wisdom tucked under your belt. I will focus on steps you can take to get a stronger head start.

2. Law students, prospective or already enrolled

Attending law school is a huge decision. From the first moments of your acceptance into law school, everyone in your life is expecting you to be a successful lawyer after you graduate. Once you start a program it is hard to stop. Legal tuition is outrageously expensive and once a student has completed a semester or two, some feel obligated to continue simply to land a job to help pay the student loans they've incurred. They feel like they can't afford to quit. If you haven't yet signed up there are significant decisions to weigh if you are applying to law school. This book will help you understand the issues not simply from the prospective of getting into law school, but a wider, longer perspective of how these decisions will impact your entire career. If you've already begun a law program, this book will give you some important things to consider as you make decisions in the coming years. This is particularly important because not all law schools are motivated to disseminate all the information necessary for students to succeed, especially the troubling information about the number of jobs that are available or the real compensation levels of the average attorney in your area. Not all law schools are great at helping you find a job after graduation. Don't worry, we're going to arm you with some helpful tips.

3. New Associates

As a freshly minted attorney who has passed the bar, you're taking the first steps into what can be a lifelong, rewarding career. You exited law school with a well-earned confidence and a bit of swagger. After you land the first job you'll soon learn that law school didn't fully prepare you for many of the decisions you'll have to make. You may not even know what questions to ask. You may not yet realize where you are starting on your firm's partnership track, or whether the track even really exists. From law school graduation to partnership is a journey of less than 8 years for most people. What you do now will impact that timeline. This book will give you tools to help you understand many of the issues that you'll face on your way to partnership.

4. Seasoned Associates

As an attorney with some experience, you may be wondering how you can maximize your chances at becoming a Partner at your firm. You will find the discussion on the Seven Year Trap insightful and it may not be too late to make some course adjustments. If you aren't seeing the progress you hoped for, you may wonder if you've made irrecoverable mistakes in your career plan. Rest assured, this book will give you much to think about. If you have a few years invested, you may have already made up your mind about how things work. I'll ask you to keep an open mind and consider some additional variables.

5. Partners and law firm management:

Yes, even Partners can learn a thing or two. Seasoned Partners would do well to refresh themselves on the numerous issues facing new lawyers. All lawyers need mentoring to maximize their potential. The most successful lawyers I know have a lifelong commitment to learning. This book contains wisdom for the benefit of the Partners as well as those who chose a career as a professional legal administrator.

Read this book in the order you want. If you are already an Associate you may want to skim or skip the first few chapters. If you are already a lawyer and you're particularly worried that you might have made some mistakes in your career you may want to jump straight into the trap chapters and then circle back.

1
Debunking Myths of the Legal Industry

If you're thinking of becoming a lawyer and you're reading this book you've already exhibited a characteristic that is a great indicator of your potential for a successful career in law. You are performing due diligence. You are researching details about an issue to formulate your own opinion. You know you need to obtain information, often from more than one source, to be able to make an informed decision. Good start.

In the profession of law, you will likely be in some form of competition every day for the rest of your life. That may sound exhausting but don't worry, you'll get used to it. You'll compete against other students to get into law school, and then against your fellow law students to achieve a better class ranking. Once you graduate, you'll compete with other job applicants to secure the position you want, and then against other lawyers as you vie for promotion. You'll be in competition with lawyers at other firms as you serve your clients. You'll also compete with yourself — pushing yourself to be the best lawyer possible. By taking the time to research the issues before you act, you've already shown that you are a step ahead of some of your peers. Of course, in this business there is always someone else who will be a step ahead of you, and that's okay. You're off to a good start but you'll learn in this book that a good start off the blocks is not enough to sustain your momentum.

Before we get too far along it makes sense to address some of the misconceptions about the legal industry. I've heard comments over the years from lawyers who wished they had a better understanding of the profession before they decided upon their career. I have lost count of the number of lawyers who confessed they had no idea about some of the fundamental issues related to working as a lawyer. Quite a few felt trapped in their situation. With no other job experience and mountains of debt from law school, some lawyers feel like they have no other options since professions outside legal won't pay them well enough to support their financial needs. Some dwell on missed opportunities. Others speak of difficulties which could have been avoided if they had only known better. Some feel they were misinformed about what life was going to be like as a lawyer. To prepare for a successful career without regret, let's start by dispelling some myths and counter them with advice.

Myth One: Becoming a lawyer will make you rich.

There is absolute truth in the statement that some lawyers make a fortune. Some work very hard and through their client development efforts they create a very successful and lucrative practice. Other lawyers are saddled with school debt and spend years, even decades, digging out. I have had many young lawyers tell me they assume they will spend the rest of their lives managing debt. They have well-paying jobs, but they are forced to live modestly because of their debt load. Still others work for the government or non-profits and make less than fast food restaurant managers. Many lawyers are solo practitioners and will never make the salaries of a Partner at a top ranked law firm. Like any profession, results vary by individuals, by firms, by specialization, and by geography. Market conditions also change frequently. Firms that are high flying one year may find themselves in a desperate financial situation a few years later.

Long standing firms can suffer catastrophic failure and collapse in a matter of months. One thing is certain though, people who pursue law as an easy way to get rich are often very disappointed with the salary or the effort that is required to earn it. Money is a lousy ultimate goal. The most miserable and paranoid person I have ever met in my life was a very powerful, wealthy attorney. Right now, at least ten miserable attorneys I know think that comment is about them specifically. A mountain of money may not matter to you if you can't stand your life, if you lose your health, or if your family and friends abandon you.

Legal salaries vary widely and there are few guarantees. Do not become a lawyer if the only reason for doing so is to become rich. If you are motivated by the money make a long term plan. Your career will have various stages. To be financially secure there are specific steps you can take at each phase to achieve the results you desire.

Myth Two: The "no life balance" stories are exaggerated.

New lawyers almost always underestimate the amount of time required to develop their career. They assume they will have to work hard, but they do not necessarily realize just how hard. Some new lawyers have never held a full-time position before they graduate law school. These people are often shocked at just how much work can be required. They may find themselves pulling all-nighters to meet a tight deadline. The realities of the profession sink in when you must stay at work while your friends in other professions get to play. It is possible to work less but those lawyers don't always keep their jobs long. Gainfully employed lawyers in private practice frequently work more than the standard 40-hour work week. Sure, it's possible to skate by, working only 9 to 5, but those lawyers rarely get promoted and are easily replaced.

There is a huge time commitment necessary to be successful in law. Most large law firms have a minimum billable requirement which is basically how many hours you have to work on projects which eventually get billed to firm clients. The common 1,900 hour annual billing requirement doesn't mean you only have to work 1,900 hours. That's how much you have to bill. And 1,900 isn't the goal — it's the minimum requirement if you want to keep your job. I'll go into the details later, but private practice is an unwise choice for people who value their free time above everything else or require flexibility to take time off without much notice. If you refuse to work any late nights or weekends, private practice may not be for you. Major life events, such as getting married and having kids, are certainly possible, but the logistics of just about everything become even more complicated in demanding professions like law, especially when you are just getting started. You'll have to manage your own life balance under these conditions. If you aren't willing to work hard law may not be the right profession for you.

Myth Three: Lawyers lead exciting lives.

They sure do — on television. For those in the real world however there is no guarantee of adventure. There are successful, jet-setting lawyers who get to do amazing work for very cool clients around the world. However, a lot of lawyers will spend all day long reviewing contracts or discovery material on a litigation matter. For some people that is exciting. For others, such work is a tedious burden. The life of a lawyer as shown on television or in the movies is almost always an exaggeration. You probably wouldn't want to watch a show featuring a lawyer engaged in 10 hours of editing contract amendments. You rarely see the TV lawyers taking an Uber home after a 16-hour day because they are too tired to drive themselves. If you want to get a real sense of what the workload can be like, talk to third or fourth year Associates. They've been in the business long enough to give you an honest assessment of the workloads at your firm. Understanding the reality of the requirements will prepare you to handle the challenges of your job.

Myth Four: You must be brilliant to be a lawyer.

Definitely not. After decades in legal administration I can personally testify that not all lawyers are brilliant. Most are great, but I've met lawyers I wouldn't trust to walk my dogs. While intelligence is very desirable in the practice of law, it's only one of the characteristics necessary to be successful. Book smarts aren't enough. Hard work, creativity, emotional intelligence and old-fashioned grit are common traits amongst successful lawyers. I've seen many very intelligent lawyers fail in firm after firm because they lack the ability to work well with others. I've met lawyers who were so completely bereft of social skills they were exiled to solo practice. You can be the smartest person in the room, but if you are a selfish jerk few people in that room are going to help you move ahead in your career. A high GPA isn't enough. The legal profession favors those who work hard, work smart, and work well with others.

Myth Five: It doesn't matter where you go to law school.

It does matter, actually. You don't have to go to an Ivy League law school to be a big-time lawyer, but it does help.

There's no question about the value of a good school, but you don't have to have a Juris Doctorate (JD) from Harvard to be successful. On the other end of the spectrum, if you choose a terrible law school, your challenges will be far greater than you can imagine. There are quite a few low performing law schools with unbelievably poor track records. These schools have a well-documented history of producing graduates with low bar examination passage rates. If you don't pass the bar, you don't practice law. Sometimes squeaking into a bad school is a worse result than not making it into law school in the first place.

Understand what you're buying before you sign up for law school. Don't settle. If you want to end up in a large law firm after graduation, research where your school's graduates landed. Check out the web pages of some of the bigger law firms. Many allow you to search their lawyer listings by law school. If you never see the school you are thinking about attending, take that into consideration. I'll talk about this in more detail later.

Myth Six: The practice of law favors old white guys.

It used to, no doubt. A lot of people assume that the legal industry is hard wired and will never change. They say that law is dominated by older white men. It is true that the senior ranks of the biggest law firms in the United States were at one time completely dominated by white males and many still are. Fortunately, the times are changing. Women and minorities have made strong inroads into most areas of law. Overt discrimination is rare these days, but some issues still remain. Most large law firms in America have embraced ethnic and gender diversity. They have their own diversity committees, support internal affinity groups, and make very public displays of their commitment. The smart firms realized long ago that diversity makes a firm stronger. The corporate world really deserves credit for driving much of the change. Most larger clients embraced and benefitted from diversity years ago.

Most firms truly want to create an environment in which everyone can succeed and contribute to the lasting success of the firm. You'll often see a section on firm websites about their commitment to diversity. Even the less enlightened firms have been forced to modernize. However, some firms are desperate to increase their minority ranks simply because their clients are demanding the change. Indeed, there is a growing list of companies who refuse to hire law firms which lack diversity. There are a few firms who simply want to increase the number of visible minorities, so they can quit failing diversity surveys and appease their clients. Want to know how to spot the difference? Just look at their partnership. It's one thing to have diversity in the lower ranks. It's very much a different thing to have inclusivity in the partnership. We've come a long way in opening doors, but there is still much to be done. I remain optimistic.

Myth Seven: The business of law is dependable and reliable.

It varies. It is true that the industry has a fairly standard playbook and some aspects of a lawyer's daily life haven't changed much. But there is risk for those firms who are not adapting or modernizing. There are rock solid firms which are well prepared for any contingency. But these are interesting times and the future may deliver even more challenges for the profession. Technology continues to change the practice of law. The way legal services are bought and sold has changed as well. Corporate clients now know how much legal services cost and have better knowledge on the topic than most law firms do. Sometimes legislative changes can impact aspects of law practice. The normal ebb and flow of the economy can have a huge impact as well. One of the biggest changes has been the consolidation of the legal industry. Firms with decades of history have vanished overnight. Anything can happen in the legal industry these days. No one is guaranteed a future. To thrive you must be adaptable and understand that change is the only constant.

2

Fair Warning: The Opinions are Opinionated

At this point some lawyers are already planning their critique of this book and we're only on the second chapter. Not everyone in the industry will agree with all my points. Some won't agree with any of them. Thoroughly researching your career options is a prudent thing to do, so it is wise to seek all opinions and not just the favorable ones. You will encounter extreme views when it comes to the topic of legal careers. Even a cursory glance at the profession will reveal hyperbole across a broad spectrum of opinions. In the viewpoint of some, a career in law is prestigious, financially rewarding, and emotionally fulfilling. To others the practice of law is a painful disappointment with unrealistic expectations and undelivered promises. There are risks in accepting the views solely from either end of the spectrum. There is bad advice from those who failed to achieve their dreams and also from those who found success easily. You should talk to as many people as possible though, even the people who have given up on law, just be mindful of the hard-wired views you will encounter.

On the negative side, there is a small army of really pissed off ex-lawyers who are utterly convinced that the legal profession is a nightmare. They have a personal mission to sway public opinion against law firm life. Before you proceed further please heed some warnings about these people and their opinions. Many of the loudest critics are people who failed in law, or at the least, they failed to meet their own expectations. They will try to convince you that you will be disappointed as well. They believe success is not possible for regular people. They have not fully reconciled their own career failings and they feel like they are striking a blow against an unjust system anytime they convince another person to adopt their views and avoid their misery.

There is no shortage of disgruntled and bitter people in the world of private law practice. The anonymity they find on the internet gives them courage to snipe from the shadows. Don't buy into their negativity. They're not performing a valued public service, they're just whining. As with everything you see and hear, it's wise to consider the source, especially when someone is pandering a sensational view with insufficient data to support their position.

It's true, some people in law do get a raw deal. There are unethical people in the industry. There are liars. There are people who are only there to feather their own nest. It's unfortunate. Never forget that experience in law varies, greatly. The vast majority of people you will encounter are ethical. They want the same things you want. They want to do an honest day's work, they want to contribute to something meaningful, and they want to be paid well for their efforts. Most will play by an ethical set of rules.

On the other end of the thought spectrum you'll find people who are entirely thrilled with law. They are often also full of crap. Don't be taken in by the Pollyannas who claim that the profession of law is without ills. Especially in academia, law is viewed in its purest, most wholesome form. It's easy to promote only the good things if you work in a laboratory environment. I can give a lecture on the finer aspects of traversing through wetlands, but you will not fully appreciate all the realities of it until you are boot deep in the swamp.

There is a strong justification for supporting the laudable aspects of the profession. The law has helped shape humanity. It governs us, protects us, unites us, and directs us. The law defends the innocent and lays assault against those who would do wrong. The law evens the playing field and removes barriers. It propels men and women to the highest ranks of our national leadership. It is easy to see why many academics are so passionate about directing young people into the field. Few professions have such high potential to create opportunities to make the world a better place. Without the rule of law, we have chaos and barbarism.

It's easy to see why opinions vary and why some people are so surprised once they become a lawyer. Law schools rarely explain just how difficult the business of law can be. Very few law schools will teach the darker side of your future career for fear of dissuading current and prospective students. Few law schools will promote their ambulance chasing alumni. These institutions survive only by recruiting new students to their ranks. Discouraging students is not something that law school personnel would ever want to do. Why? Because they too have to act like a business. Even non-profits need financial support. Without students paying tuition, these programs would disappear.

Anyone can learn the law — but not everyone will be a good lawyer and not everyone can make a career of it. Not all share the same definition of success. A career in law requires much more time, effort, and sacrifice than most people realize. It's worth mentioning early that the experiences in law vary wildly and some of the factors are far beyond your control. Even the best prepared new lawyers can find themselves in tough situations like recessions. I'll talk about the power of the overall economy soon.

You'll have no control over that ocean, but you may be able to pick which waves you'll ride.

You will soon learn that every firm and every area of practice concentration has its own unique aspects. If you develop a practice in a very complicated, unique niche of the industry you may work on infrequent, but highly profitable projects. If you work for a firm that does something like insurance defense work, you may have endless high volume/low margin work opportunities. One of the first things that you will notice is that the volume of work you will do does not necessarily correlate to higher profits. You will see some people who appear to toil for little reward, and others who make finding quick and profitable projects seem effortless. Some firms have unfailing supplies of work and opportunities to shine. Other firms have such a narrow focused and limited organizational chart that you have no shot at advancement. At times it may feel unfair. The disparity can be broad, so the experiences of the Associates down the hall in another practice group may be completely different than yours. Worse yet, you and your peers in those other sections are likely to be evaluated by a single system of measurement. The inequity can feel discriminatory, but often it's just the business realities of a particular practice. Where the gaps are wide, some people feel their situation is unfair, and those feelings create strong opinions and reactions.

Not everyone will walk lock-step down the same path. As a new Associate a few of your colleagues will start off with some advantages you won't have. Some will come with professional work experience in other industries. Others start with more exposure to legal or business issues because they continued their education beyond law school and earned an LLM, CPA, MBA, or advanced engineering degree. Some will be the children or grandchildren of successful lawyers and they may begin with more knowledge or contacts than you. Not everyone will fit nicely into the same box, so be warned that your situation may not turn out exactly as described in law school, during your new hire orientation, or even as shown in this book.

This industry can chew up people who aren't prepared for the pressure involved. A quick word of caution on the pressure which can occur in this profession. Some lawyers will struggle with stress, depression, or dependency disorders. A recent study by the American Bar Association (ABA) and the Hazelden Betty Ford Foundation highlighted the real threats to attorneys. Even if you never have these issues personally, odds are you will encounter someone who does. Some lawyers find themselves in very difficult situations and the stress can seem overwhelming at times. There are resources available to assist people in need every step of the way, from counselors at law school, to well-being committees at your local bar association, to employee assistance programs (EAP) at your employer. If you ever think you may need help, please ask for it.

3

Everything in the Legal World is Changing

Many of the seasoned lawyers you will meet will have a mindset planted firmly in the past, in a time when the legal industry was different. They grew up during a period when technology had not yet replaced many of the aspects in their profession. Changes occurred back then, but the pace of change was slower. Many law firms reluctantly accepted change and only did so because their clients forced the issue. I recall a time when WordPerfect's word processing software still dominated law firms despite the fact that most of the business world had embraced Microsoft Word. At the time WordPerfect had much better formatting features. Legal secretaries did all the document drafting and they loved WordPerfect. Clients' usage of Word created continual problems and discussions about document conversions and backward capabilities of various versions. Once, when a client complained because they couldn't open our document, one of our lawyers commented that the client needed to get a better software package. Such a callous disregard of client needs is a rare thing these days.

Many law firms operated without significant changes for years. It was not uncommon for major law firms to work with antiquated tools and old versions of software which were no longer even supported. Back then the billable hour was king, and lawyers billed seemingly limitless hours on client projects. Every year firms would raise their standard billing rates and most clients wouldn't blink. Lawyers spent a lot of time at the office and made good money, but not obscene money. Life for most law firms was predictable.

This is important to realize because there are several generations of lawyers in practice today. The senior attorneys remember the days before email, databases, and predictive analytics. They remember the days when they didn't have to share a secretary with four other lawyers. Some will try to convince you that the old ways are still the best ways. They may have been very successful developing clients in the 1980s and they wonder why you aren't approaching business development like they did. They may still believe their approaches are the only legitimate way to do business. Many of them spent long hours at the office because they had to be there to get the work done. There were few remote work opportunities. If you aren't following the steps as they did, they may think you are on the wrong path.

Prior to technological advancements, most problems were solved by deploying manpower. In litigation matters the lawyers would set up war rooms to handle large cases. When document production occurred, couriers would drop off stacks of banker boxes packed with documents. A team of lawyers and paralegals would painstakingly review every page, manually numbering each document with the steady click of a mechanical Bate Stamp, indexing everything on a master list. Law was paper intensive and fingertip papercuts were a common hazard for everyone.

Technology has changed everything. The production scenario above can now be handled electronically. All the documents are scanned and imported into litigation support software. Predictive analytic software sifts through the mountain of data, producing information which a lawyer can review at their desk, or on a laptop from the comfort of their own home. Hours of physical work is replaced by a single mouse click. Although many lawyers still hold on to stacks of papers, the typical office these days is no longer a fire hazard.

How we gather and manage information has changed forever. A great example is something we take for granted now — simply being able to identify other lawyers. For years Martindale Hubble was the powerhouse index of all attorneys around the world. The company spent an incredible amount of time recording where lawyers worked and published hard back books which held this information. In the pre-internet world if you needed an attorney in another jurisdiction where you didn't know anyone, you would go down to your firm's law library and find an entire section of Martindale Hubble books. There were books for every country and as you might imagine, they were likely out of date moments after they were printed. Back then lawyers stayed at their firms longer, so the model was good enough. Now their service is listed online, and the entire database is timely and accessible with little effort. The same goes for research. In the past printed books filled lavish libraries and lined the hallways of law firms. Library staff were plentiful and there were small squads of assistants charged with constantly adding updated pages or inserts to ensure that the books contained the latest information. Research is mostly online now, and the once grand law libraries are an anachronistic relic of the previous generation. Lease space is generally the second largest expense of a law firm. With no need for stacks of books, the old library spaces have been repurposed. Often the rows of leather-bound law books are present only for aesthetic effect.

Advancements in legal technology have created some strange contradictions. In litigation practices, widespread adoption of sophisticated discovery and case management software has not democratized access to the court system. The ability to quickly gather and analyze millions of points of information has actually increased the costs of litigation because firms are required to maintain complex systems and personnel to manage the mountains of data. With arbitration and mediation costs increasing, some clients simply do the math to determine an acceptable settlement amount rather than hassle with an actual trial. The number of jury trials has been declining for years. Many senior lawyers are adept at e-discovery software yet their experience in an actual trial is minimal.

A variety of significant changes hit the U.S. legal market in the last three decades, from rapid technological advances in the 1980s and 1990s, to serious economic shocks, leading to changes in client demand and buying habits. The biggest change in recent years started in 2008. Economic downturns can wreak havoc on the industry. In 2008–2009 the global economy hit a rough patch which would eventually be labeled the "Great Recession." Just a year before most firms were wildly optimistic. The industry was too bullish. Convinced of the never-ending supply of profitable work, some law firms became aggressive in opening new offices and securing the best talent they could afford. At the time, the standard starting annual compensation for first year Associates at larger law firms increased from $140,000 to $160,000. Business was so strong that some firm leaders were starting to talk about the next jump to $180,000 or even $200,000 to outprice the weaker competitors. The economy was humming, and people were optimistic. But then it all stopped.

When the housing bubble burst and the mortgage crisis hit in late 2008, U.S. subprime mortgage failures peaked, credit tightened around the world, and a banking crisis ensued, all of which contributed to the recession. Risky investments fell through, thousands of mortgages began to go into default, and the economic dominos started to fall in the world of legal services. Clients put a break on pending legal work and suddenly the entire legal market seemed to grind to a halt. With revenue streams turned off and no clear indications on when the work would resume, law firms did what they always do in stressful economic times — they turned toward expenses. Compensation is their largest expenditure and with dropping workloads, law firms had no choice but to lay lawyers off — and they did by the thousands. 2008–2009 saw a purge in the legal industry as firm after firm began to cut their ranks. Daily announcements of layoffs continued for week after week. Websites began to track the carnage. Many firms cancelled their summer clerkship programs and even rescinded the job offers they had made to graduating law students. For many firms this wasn't simply a measure to ensure they hit a certain profit level, it was a drastic action to ensure they could pay the rent and stay in business. Not all survived.

Of course, the industry recovered. Even bad situations can create a positive outcome for some people. As we fell on hard times in 2008, new lawyers had amazingly different experiences depending on their practice area. Real estate lawyers were battered because the number of transactions in their sections fell to staggeringly low numbers. The bankruptcy folks fared much better as demand for their services skyrocketed. Good law firms, as well as good lawyers, are adaptable and resilient. After decades of being shielded from many realities of the business world, the recession made law firms realize that they had to play by the same rules as their clients. Don't ever forget that this is a long term play — so if you hang in there, bad situations often yield back to the good. Even those real estate lawyers who took a beating survived. When the economy eventually recovered a few years later there was a huge demand for young real estate attorneys. The demand was high because the supply of talent was low. Those who survived the downturn were in a strong position when the markets rebounded. The legal industry lags just behind the primary economy in the U.S., lurching from peak to trough to peak again.

Recessions are not uncommon in America, but the economic downturn of 2008 and 2009 left some permanent marks. Not all of the lessons have been carved in stone, but the industry made some significant changes. The main difference was in the way large corporate clients purchased legal services. For decades the primary manner on which law firms billed their services was through hourly billing. Giving a cost estimate wasn't the normal approach, but after the 2008 recession hit more clients began to demand predictability on their legal expenditures. Facing tough times, many firms began to embrace alternate fee arrangements (AFA). They offered flat fee estimates and a variety of creative billing approaches to combat clients' concerns about hourly billing. AFAs never took over completely as some predicted, but the demand for certainty in legal expenditures stuck. Even those firms which resisted AFAs were forced to pay more attention to their own work product and the amounts they charged for services.

The industry recovered and became even more competitive. The biggest threat to some firms is no longer market conditions but rather other firms raiding them and recruiting away their Partners. Stealing talent and clients from other firms can be the fastest way to grow a law firm. There has been continuous merger movement in the legal industry during the last decade, with hundreds of mergers in the U.S. market. For an in-depth look at the volume of these transactions I recommend Altman Weil's Mergerline website. This legal consulting firm has done a good job capturing the details of many of the mergers that have occurred over the years. I'll discuss this in more depth later.

The hunt for business has also produced a need to secure the best talent to help retain that business. Law firm pay at the largest firms continues to climb, putting more pressure on mid-sized firms. It's a cat and mouse game, where the larger firms make tactical moves in compensation knowing full well that most of their competitors will attempt to match their pay scales, even if they can't afford to do so. Firms feel pressured because they can't risk losing their high-performing talent.

The competitive nature of the legal market is at times deviously brilliant and the nationwide compensation matching exercise is a great example. The firms who decide to increase first year Associate compensation don't announce it ahead of time. They don't move when everyone else is still planning their annual budget. They quietly plan for their own cost increases and then spring an announcement on the marketplace at some point during the year. Most other firms have not budgeted for the increase, so matching the new comp range means a drastic cut to their own annual profitability. Why is it drastic? The last few increases have been $20,000 for first year lawyers, but firms can't simply raise the starting salary for first year lawyers only, because that would mean first years might make more than some second-year attorneys. The raises hit the entire Associate pool, costing some firms millions of dollars.

Firms have tried to cope with these pressures by coming up with some fairly creative ways to get more from their Associates to help offset the rising costs. Some have created modifications to the Partner promotion track to allow for a slower path, thus slowing compensation expectations. Some have made the raises contingent on performance. It's a game of money ball and the richer firms are almost always the winner. Smaller firms have to be even smarter now to compete.

Take a moment to think about the current state of the legal market. Every year another 40,000 to 50,000 new lawyers join the marketplace. Attorneys who used to retire at 65 now regularly work into their 70s. Technology has fundamentally reduced the amount of time necessary to do legal work. Clients have become savvy consumers of legal services, leveraging their own tech resources and buying power. So, there we have our industry: more lawyers, flat growth in legal services demanded, spiraling costs. No one said this was going to be easy.

4
Pre-Law Considerations

For those of you thinking about law school read on. If you are already a lawyer, you can skip or skim the next few chapters. Or you can read them to either validate your past decisions or get a deeper insight into how things may be changing.

I've met many students, some in their early teens, who were convinced they would someday be a lawyer. In college or university an undergrad student will eventually declare their major focus of study. We know people often change their majors as time passes and they gain exposure to new areas of thought. This is perfectly acceptable and even desirable. As you experience new things it makes sense that your broadened awareness of the world will present new and exciting opportunities.

People who hear the calling to law their senior year of high school can be tempted to start their studies early by enrolling in a degree program specifically designed to prepare you for a career as a lawyer. Indeed, several schools offer pre-law programs, or other degree programs with a pre-law component. There is some debate about the value of an undergraduate focus on the study of law. These pre-law programs aren't available at all schools, in part because many feel the degree concentration has limited value. Those institutions that offer these programs claim they allow for a deeper understanding of the law, which can lead to better results when it comes to law school admission. Maybe they're right, but maybe not.

One reason there are so few of these pre-law programs is because pre-law undergraduate degree programs have not been warmly embraced by the legal community. A common view is that they fail to encourage a broad enough range of study. Law school acceptance committees want to see candidates with a depth and breadth of learning. An undergraduate degree with a focus on English and writing courses will support your career much more than a few introductory courses on jurisprudence. A good philosophy course may help you develop more sophisticated critical reasoning skills than you might develop through an undergraduate course on legal issues.

When it comes to the value of these programs certainly not all schools are equal and consequently not all pre-law programs produce the same result. The American Bar Association is the largest legal professional association in the world and has been around since the 1870s. They set the standards for the industry and provide accreditation for law schools. The ABA has no approved curriculum for pre-law study programs.

You don't need to do a pre-law degree program to connect with the industry. There are numerous pre-law societies, professional associations, organizations and other programs found at universities around the country that exist outside of an actual pre-law degree program. While these other options may encourage or even require participation in a certain core of classes, they don't detract from the broader curriculum of the school. These programs often focus on the practical realities of the profession and frequently create opportunities to connect with professionals in the industry itself. Such connections are valuable and hard to make when just starting out.

The first four years of your education do not need to be and should not be entirely focused on the law. Taking basic business courses is always a smart option because they will help you understand the issues of your future clients. Knowing the basic concepts of accounting, marketing, and operations can provide valuable knowledge that will serve you for a lifetime. Government and civics courses will help you understand the legislative and judicial process. Speech and debate classes can provide experience with public speaking and presentation skills. Rest assured whatever you focus on in an accredited university will not hurt your prospects for entry into law school if you do well in your studies. Your grade point average is one of the things that a law school will look at when considering your admission request, but it's only one aspect. If you do not excel as an undergraduate student, you may find your path a little harder. The best advice is to find something you enjoy, and then throw yourself into it fully.

One of the most important skills you can learn is how to write well. Writing skills are critical in the practice of law. Poor writing can be what prevents a clerk from receiving a job offer as an Associate, or what keeps an Associate from being promoted to Partner. It is exceedingly difficult to advance in the legal world without strong writing and grammar skills. At some point during your job search as an Associate it is very likely that the firm you want to work for will ask for your resume and a writing sample. I have personally seen substandard writing skills listed as the reason to pass on a candidate.

It doesn't matter if you're writing a court brief or simple correspondence with a client, it's all important. Even a poorly written email in the office can make some senior attorneys worry about using you in the future. As a young law clerk, you will be given many research projects and you'll be asked to write memos of the key concepts. This exercise is used not only to see if you can grasp the key elements of the law, it's designed to showcase your writing skills to those who are supervising you. Produce a series of terrible memos and you'll have with fewer opportunities. You can make life easier down the road by learning how to write well.

The legal world is full of examples that warn of the perils for those who have not mastered grammar. Take for example the well-known case commonly known as the Comma Rule Case, which pitted cable giant Rogers Communications of Toronto, Canada, against Bell Aliant, a telephone company located in the Canadian Maritimes. The entire case boiled down to a provision in the contract regarding automatic renewal provisions and Bell Aliant's ability to terminate the agreement. The phrase in question might seem simple at first glance:

> "This agreement shall be effective from the date it is made and shall continue in force for a period of five (5) years from the date it is made, and thereafter for successive five (5) year terms, unless and until terminated by one year prior notice in writing by either party."

Because of the placement of the final comma, Bell argued it could cancel its contract earlier than what Rogers desired. Rogers believed the contract required a five-year commitment. Bell Aliant read it and determined they could get out with only one-year prior notice, and they wanted out. In an initial review, Federal regulators reviewed the contract and concluded that the second comma related to the one-year notice for cancellation applied to both the five-year term and the renewal term.

Effectively, that additional comma gave Aliant an escape clause in the contract after just one year.

The fight continued but Rogers prevailed in the end after much argument over grammar and comma placements, complete with lengthy opinions submitted by grammar experts. In the end a French version of the exact same contract helped Rogers win the point with regulators. The entire case was a tremendous drain of time and resources. It could have all been avoided.

When you are ready to check out law schools start by looking for an ABA accredited law school. As you begin your research into schools you'll soon hear of each school's rankings. Do a little research on rankings because not all are legitimate. The American Bar Association is not in the ranking business nor does it want to be. They make that point clear in their own materials:

> "Neither the American Bar Association nor its Section of Legal Education and Admissions to the Bar endorses, cooperates with, or provides data to any law school ranking system. Several organizations rank or rate law schools; however, the ABA provides only a statement of accreditation status. No ranking or rating system of law schools is attempted or advocated by the ABA. Prospective law students should consider a variety of factors in making their choice among schools."

Be wary of law school bias in the rankings you might see. Attending a top ranked school is not an absolute requirement for a successful career in law. If you want a good idea about how a specific law school has really performed, just check out where their alumni end up. You may also want to check some of the free data that is available from the American Bar Association. If you dig a bit, you'll find some interesting information.

One thing that you need to consider is the total cost of the programs you are considering. A review of the 2013 graduates of the University of Chicago School of Law showed that 85% graduated with school debt. Their average debt was $156,753. What's sad about these numbers is the fact that the University of Chicago didn't even rank as the highest debt per student that year. The mounting U.S. debt attributed to educational loans has reached record heights. If your school finance plan includes loans for both undergrad and law school, you will enter the workforce with an unholy mountain of debt. Carrying a huge debt can force some people to stay in positions they hate because they have no other choice. Worse are those who don't make enough money to properly service their debt. They are trapped. Those federally backed student loans have some hefty strings attached and there is a virtual ocean of loan-collecting privateers just waiting for a letter of marque with your name on it. If you default on your loans you will be mercilessly pursued by collectors, and in the end, this can add even more to your burden if you are saddled with processing fees. You can be sued. Your wages can be held. The law allows for a garnishment of 15% of your disposable pay, meaning that your debt will be repaid one way or another for as long as it takes.

Plan accordingly. Discuss family support, pursue grants and scholarships, save in advance, don't blow your money on stupid things, and live by a budget. If your entire strategy on handling your debt is to simply make a ton of money after you graduate, you need to stop and think about what your situation will look like if you hit a detour on your road to a high-paying job. I'm going to address the realities of legal pay in more detail soon.

As you start to think about law school or begin a program, there are other things you can do at this stage to help increase your odds of success. For starters, meet as many people as possible when you are in school. Start to grow your professional network now. As an undergrad you can join the future-lawyer or pre-law program at your school. Talk to your school's career counselors about jobs in the legal field. Some schools support mentoring programs which can match you up with a professional.

It might even be possible to find a part-time administrative position with a law firm, which can be a good option if you need a bit more money; but enter it with realistic expectations. First, try to avoid any position which detracts from your studies. As a student your main focus needs to be school. Second, while the first-hand insight you'll receive by working in a law firm is great, your experiences as an entry-level administrative employee are not likely to produce high level mentoring and guidance. That level of connection with students usually only occurs with law students participating in the firm's official summer clerkship program. Traditionally, there is a great deal of turnover with entry level positions, so most firms are unlikely to invest serious career mentoring to help you someday become a lawyer. Not many lawyers will take a file clerk or receptionist under their wing and help guide them into a career in law.

If you are a young student, you can still gain experience now that will be attractive to law schools. You can show your leadership attributes by becoming engaged in civic and charitable organizations. There is no downside to this type of involvement. Working with a reputable charity will help you meet more people and you might even learn some skills along the way. Meet everyone you can and be nice to them because some of them will remain contacts for the rest of your life. Student groups and professional associations are great organizations to join. If your university does not have a pre-law association you have just stumbled upon your first leadership opportunity. With the help of faculty advisors, you could help create your school's pre-law student organization. This is a great way to dip your feet into leadership. You'll meet other students and professors and add them to your network of contacts. You may create opportunities to interact with the professional community as well. Pre-law societies frequently find judges or lawyers willing to present to their groups. There are many legal professionals who will take time to share their wisdom. This is a great method to meet and create permanent connections with people already in the business.

Think about your résumé as it will look after graduation. If you take the traditional approach your résumé will show that you have an undergraduate degree and participated in a few extracurricular activities. It might even show that you had some low-level part time work. That's not bad, but it won't necessarily land you a job. Contrast this with the résumé of someone who has been very active during their four years at college. This individual might have one full of experiences with numerous charitable organizations. These experiences will help differentiate you from other similarly situated students. If you focus some time and effort each year of your undergrad degree towards a separate charitable institution by the time you graduate you'll have four-line items on your résumé, with stories to tell about each and valuable references from each organization. It's helpful to have multiple references who are willing to vouch for your character, intelligence, and work ethic. There is an ongoing debate about how much time should be spent on studies and how much time should be spent on extracurricular activities. There really isn't a right or wrong answer in most cases. Don't forget that the sum of your experiences will tell a story about your potential. Keep up your GPA, but live life and try to broaden your range of experiences. Whenever possible you want your résumé to tell a compelling story. Sometimes even a single line on a résumé can spark a conversation. In college I worked part time for the Walt Disney Company. While this job was not the pinnacle of my career, early on it caught the attention of people interviewing me.

Don't forget that your career is a marathon, not a sprint. Don't pressure yourself to do too much, too soon. At the start of your career no admission counselor or potential employer is expecting to see a long list of professional successes on your résumé, but they want to see something. They need to see who you are to get an idea of who you will become. Early in your career you get hired based on attitude and aptitude. It takes years to master a trade.

At the start of your career you'll get hired because people like you and see your potential. They believe you'll be a good cultural fit with their organization. This is why an active undergraduate experience is helpful. If you can show initiative and effort early on, you're a step ahead of everyone else. If your résumé simply says you graduated, you'll have to work harder to convince potential employers why you are worthy of employment.

It's worth a pause to pound this point. By virtue of your undergraduate degree the business world owes you exactly nothing. Getting an undergrad degree is an accomplishment you should be proud of. A lot of people will never reach this level of education. You should be proud of it, but don't get cocky. Graduating with a BA from a great college does not guarantee you a corner office with a secretary and a reserved parking spot. In professional circles of many industries the undergrad degree doesn't open doors — it's a mandatory minimum threshold you must cross even to reach the door.

The degree itself won't set you apart from others. Your character will. Consider two people, one whose parents paid for their four-year education and another student who worked his or her way through school taking five or six years to complete their undergraduate education. Who has the better story in the eyes of a recruiter? It depends on the recruiter. The student who took longer has an opportunity to turn their challenge into a great story. Why? Because that second person was not simply handed their opportunity on a platter, they fought for it. Students who have 100% of their way paid for them often spend four years completely detached from the reality of adult life. Some may have great stories from Spring Break but nothing to offer in terms of real world experience. In the real world our rent isn't paid for us, we don't get a spending allowance, and our car insurance gets cancelled if we don't make a payment. In the real world if you don't have a paycheck you don't get to buy groceries.

Your personal starting point does not limit the destinations you can reach. The candidates who worked hard to get where they are may have a leg up in some interview situations because their success only occurred because of their efforts and determination. They can tell the story of their journey and demonstrate their tenacity and grit. They can show how they didn't shrink from a challenge. They can talk about how they overcame adversities. These are all laudable characteristics that employers appreciate because it shows them that you are prepared for the rigors of the real world. Remember, at the start of your career few people get hired because of their experience. They get hired because of their personalities, their character, and the potential that resides within. They get hired because they are a good fit.

With a well-rounded undergraduate education taken care of, you'll start to look at the many options for law school. You'll need to gather information because you have a lot to consider.

5

The Bad Law School Trap

There is a trap that can kill your legal career before it even starts. As you start to explore various law schools there are certain ones you should avoid like the plague. Whatever you do, don't give any consideration to the vast majority of unaccredited law schools out there. Odds are the state you live in doesn't even permit these schools to operate, but a few states, such as California, do allow them. If a school is unaccredited, it means that the ABA has not approved their program. Attending an unaccredited law school can be very risky, very expensive, and very frustrating.

There is only one situation where I would ever recommend attendance at an unaccredited school. New law schools are not instantly approved by the ABA. They need at least one year before they become accredited. Occasionally, a university without a law program will acquire a smaller private law school. If that occurs accreditation should be a snap. If a large well-established university launches a new law school, they will go through a period of provisional approval first. There may be some minor complications, but presumably a large university system will not let their new law school go under. You would expect them to deploy all necessary resources to ensure their school's success, so a provisional situation may resolve itself in quick order.

That's it. Avoid the rest of them. Almost all other schools which are not approved by the ABA have a much lower success rate than accredited schools. These private, unaccredited law schools should be scrutinized with tremendous wariness. Most people try to judge a law school's success by checking out what percentage of their graduates pass the bar examination. Don't stop at the bar, dig deeper and you'll see how terrible some of these schools really are. In 2015 a *Los Angeles Times* investigation revealed that nearly 9 out of 10 students in unaccredited law schools in California drop out. 9 out of 10! An article about this investigation followed a student named Omar Medina and chronicled his experience with Northwestern California University School of Law. Medina, a security officer, sought a part-time online program which was flexible enough to complete while still allowing time for work and family. After paying about $3,000 for tuition, he dropped out after two years of struggling with the program.

"They aren't even diploma mills, they are failure factories," said Robert Fell with the University of San Diego School of Law in the *Times* interview. Fell, like others from accredited law schools, criticize these unaccredited programs and their dismal track records. You might expect schools to knock their competition, but in this case the legitimate schools are offering their critiques not because they are afraid of the competitors. They are afraid that substandard schools derail students and cheapen the profession.

Northwestern California bills itself as an institution with "World Class Education in Law." The school offers online "real-time" text, chats, and videoconference sessions in the school's virtual classroom. You should not pick a law school based on how easy it is to get in to or how simple it is to complete the program. Good programs don't deliver critical learning materials via text messages.

You really do get what you pay for. Tuition at Northwestern California University School of Law is less than $4,000 a year. By comparison, tuition at Baylor Law School in Texas is about $60,000 a year. Baylor has a long and successful history, boasting bar passage rates which are typically 10 to 15% better than the state average. Their grads have high employment rates. Yes, the cost to attend is significantly higher, but most people in that program can boast a strong return on their investment.

Graduating from a non-accredited school will not impress many law firm recruiters. The truth is that many of them don't view these programs as legitimate. You also won't end up with the benefit of a powerful alumni network. Part of the advantage of any good school is the quality and breadth of the people you will meet while attending, people who share your alma mater. You will graduate with an entire class of business contacts. Your school's alumni network can be an invaluable source of connections and opportunities. If you attend a school where the entire curriculum is presented online, you shouldn't expect to make the same level of connection that would happen in a traditional classroom-based program.

Some of these schools have good intentions and try earnestly to earn accreditation. Others prey on the uninformed and take advantage of people who are so desperate to attend law school that they'll sign up assuming they have nothing to lose. Regardless of their intentions, it's the outcome that matters. There are no shortcuts for important professions like the law. If a program sounds too good to be true, it probably is. *Caveat Emptor*.

Technically, it is possible to attend one of these schools, pass the bar, and then become a gainfully employed lawyer. There are a few success stories, but the odds are stacked against you. Many of these schools promote the companies which employ their graduates. Do your research and you'll see that some of those folks are not employed in a position that requires a JD. If you truly want to see what your outcome at one of these programs might look like, go to LinkedIn and search for former graduates of any of these schools. You will probably find that most are not working in the type of position you would like to have. If you plan on working at a large law firm this is definitely not the way to go. Focus all your energy on getting into the best school possible.

6

Getting in to a Good Law School

In 2018, 49 of the top 50 law schools in the U.S. had acceptance rates less than 50%. The top ten law schools accepted less than 18.5% of their total applicants. Law schools want the best students possible and there is no shortage of candidates for them to consider. The average undergraduate GPA for students accepted into the top ten law schools was 3.83. That's the average — on the higher end at the seventy-fifth percentile of students accepted into the top ten programs, the average GPA was 3.918. If you want to get into Yale, Stanford, Harvard, University of Chicago, or Columbia, or any other top tier school, you're going to have to meet some very tough standards. On the other end of the spectrum are schools with fewer top ranked applicants and higher acceptance rates. The Thomas M. Cooley Law School in Florida has the dubious honor of having one of the highest acceptance rates in the country. For the 2016–2017 school year Cooley Law had 1,067 applicants and they accepted 915. Their 85% acceptance rate is not normal. Is that a problem? Probably. In a recent bar examination almost half of their graduates failed.

Law schools consider numerous aspects before they approve a student for admission. Admission is a competition. There are only 204 accredited schools (meaning their curriculum is approved by the American Bar Association) in the United Sates and each year between 45,000 and 55,000 applicants seek admission. There are more applicants than there are available positions. Because of this competitive situation many students apply to more than one program. A considerable number will apply to five or more programs.

The ABA prepares a "509 Information Report" for all accredited law schools. These reports are available online on the ABA website. In one quick report you can learn a tremendous amount of information about any law school. It's all there: application acceptance rates, tuition, demographic breakdowns — all the information you might want right down to the bar passage rates. As an undergrad you can find other great resources through your school's academic and career advisory department, or a pre-law society. There is also a mountain of information available from the law schools themselves.

There are a great many factors that law schools consider when they look at applicants to their program. They want to sign up students who will add to the school's legacy. Law schools try to get as much information as feasible on candidates to determine if they have the right stuff. Admission is a competitive process and your personality, background, academic and personal accomplishments will be considered. Before you start papering law schools around the country with your application, you'll want to understand the process and develop a methodical approach to your admission strategy. Each school has its own unique process. Start your research by reviewing law school websites.

To gain entrance into the majority of law schools, you'll likely have to complete the Law School Admission Test (LSAT), which is a half-day, standardized test required for admission to most law schools. The LSAT is prepared and administered by the Law School Admission Council (LSAC). There are good resources available through the LSAC website. Despite what you might hear about the waning importance of this test, it's still the single biggest thing that will help you get into a good school. If you want to go to law school, you really can't avoid taking this test. If finding a way to avoid the test is a major component of your law school entrance strategy you may want to reconsider your plans. Don't try to game the system. There are good reasons why the test exists so if you skip it you'll find fewer options as you move forward.

It is strongly advised that you take the LSAT in the summer of the year preceding the year in which you plan to apply for admission. When you are applying to law school you want to present your application early in the process, so you don't want to be waiting on grades. You can register with the LSAC's Credential Assembly Service (CAS) to get into the testing system. Registration for the CAS can be accomplished at the same time you register for the LSAT. The LSAC will send your testing results to the law schools to which you wish to apply. Please note that LSAC will not send any law school a report until they have received transcripts from every undergraduate institution you have attended, including summer sessions and semesters abroad. You also must pay any necessary fees before they'll send anything on your behalf. Again, you don't want to delay or make rookie mistakes in the application process, so make sure you pay attention to each school's requirements.

Not all law schools require the LSAT, but most do. Some schools weigh the results more than others. The Massachusetts School of Law places more emphasis on interviewing candidates and announces their opinion of the LSAT clearly on their admission page:

"Also, because of the considerable criticisms of the LSAT, Massachusetts School of Law does not consider the LSAT when making admissions decisions. Instead, it considers an essay test that the school itself has developed and most importantly, it is read and graded by a full time MSLAW professor who, based upon years of practical and academic experience, is well qualified to assess an applicant's ability to think and write well. The requirement of a mandatory interview, the review of an applicant's entire record in school and the work force, and the essay aptitude test enable the Admissions Committee to identify worthy students who would be denied admission to traditional law schools simply because of their LSAT scores."

Most law schools place value on the information they receive from prospective student's LSAT score because it provides them with a deeper insight into the student's reading ability and reasoning skills. It doesn't measure a person's knowledge of the law, it measures their aptitude for learning it. The admission teams at law schools will receive more applicants than the positions available, consequently they need to cull the applicant pool. The LSAT is a tool they use to thin the herd.

The test itself is considered by many to be quite difficult. Those who attempt it will write for 3½ hours, answering multiple choice questions. There is a half hour essay section. Reading comprehension is shown by answering questions on short narratives. There are also sections testing your comparative reasoning ability and your logical analytical reasoning skills.

So how do you best prepare for the big test? There is an entire industry built around preparing students for the LSAT. You can purchase any number of books, videos, sample tests, and comprehensive review courses to help you prepare for it. You will find more than 1,000 LSAT prep books listed on Amazon.

Many students will take preparation courses to increase their odds of performing well. One of the preparation companies offers programs ranging from $650 to $1,200 depending on the length of the class. Many people will argue in favor of these programs. The logic is sound. If you are willing to spend more than $100K to get a law degree, why not pay another thousand to ensure that you get into the best possible school?

LSAT scores range from 120 to 180. If you want to get into the top 50 law schools in the United States, you need to score 160 or higher. While the LSAT isn't the sole determining factor at many schools, there is no question about the value of a high score. A high score will never hurt. A low score can ruin your chances. While Yale considers LSAT scores, it does not have a threshold score for consideration. The class of 2016 had a median score of 173. Harvard requires the LSAT, citing it as a helpful tool to help them sort through applications. Their median LSAT is also 173. Their view: "in the context of the broader range of information contained in a complete application for admission, the LSAT is helpful in assessing individual promise and in making meaningful comparisons among those who apply for admission."

Law schools look at each applicant carefully. Some students will find themselves with the "splitter" designation, meaning that your LSAT score and undergrad GPA don't correlate as expected. That means you have a good GPA and the LSAT was below par, or your GPA is weak and you nailed the LSAT. You'll hear various iterations of the terms and lots of opinions on what it means or what it doesn't mean. At this point in the process your grades are what they are.

Schools can change their admission criteria. In addition to taking the LSAT, you'll have to fill out law school applications. Almost all the top law programs charge a fee to submit your application. Stanford's application fee is currently $100, while the South University Law Center in Baton Rouge Louisiana is a bargain at only $50. Many schools do not require an application fee. There may be some correlation to the fees charged and the popularity of the university, but don't read too much into this. This is simply a method law schools use to control costs and limit admission consideration to those prospective students who are serious about applying. The fee is a barrier of entry to knock out people who are unwilling to invest even a nominal amount to show their true interest. Obviously, if the process were free some of the best schools would be overwhelmed by students who aren't particularly interested or don't have a realistic chance but would consider going if they could somehow work their way into a top tier school. There is also a group of prospective students who feel the need to send their details to as many schools as possible hoping to increase their odds by the sheer number of applications submitted.

Some programs require a letter of recommendation and others make it optional. If you can submit a letter you should do it. Some programs seek a letter from an academic reference and one from a business or community service organization. If you are now realizing that you don't have anyone willing to write you a letter it's probably wise to start working on this as a goal.

Admission committees can't help but see value in the heartfelt letters which provide examples of your better qualities. Submitting the letters will help, especially if you have several sources willing to write a letter. Letters from professors, civic leaders, and business people who have seen you in action are valuable. Remember, your entire admission package will be reviewed, and you are up against other students who want your seat in the program. The stronger the application the better.

Most application packets require a letter or statement of interest. This is a great opportunity to promote who you are and explain why you really want to earn the degree. These programs don't have to settle. They seek the best students who will help maintain their standards and contribute to their success. You should explain not only why you want to be a lawyer, you also need to tell them why you want to be a lawyer who graduated from their particular school. It's your chance to convince them that you will be a great alumnus someday.

The statement letter allows you a shot to differentiate yourself from other students. The school will provide you plenty of examples of what they are looking for. To get a flavor of the expectations and requirements, check out the approaches from these three law schools:

"An applicant must submit a personal statement on any subject of importance that he or she feels will assist the Admissions Committee in its decision. It should be no more than two pages, double-spaced. Applicants may also submit an optional statement discussing characteristics and accomplishments they believe will contribute positively to the GW Law community and to the legal profession." — George Washington School of Law

"A personal statement is required and must be electronically attached to the application for admission. It should not exceed two pages and may provide the Admissions Committee with information regarding such matters as intellectual interests and pursuits; personal, family or educational background, experiences and talents of special interest, reasons for applying to law school as they may relate to personal goals and professional expectations, or any other factors that will assist the committee's evaluation of the applicant's candidacy for admission. Applicants also may describe, either within the personal statement or as an addendum, how their admission would contribute to the diversity of the College of Law." — Depaul University School of Law

"The essay should be used to provide information about yourself that you consider significant to our evaluation of your file. For that reason, general essays on the justice system are not particularly useful or helpful to your chances for admission, nor do we recommend that you simply repeat information provided elsewhere in your application. We want to learn what makes you tick, why you are someone we should want to enroll at Tulane. We are interested in learning about those of your qualities that would be valuable to the legal profession, the law school classroom, and the community. You may wish to describe a significant experience in your life or to discuss your interest in or motivation for attending law school. Avoid using your essay to explain problems with your academic, LSAT, or conduct record, but do ensure that these matters are addressed-preferably in separate enclosures. You are also encouraged to provide, separate from your essay, explanations of factors you feel are relevant to our evaluation of your file." — Tulane University Law School

Do you see what they are looking for? Perhaps the best advice on Personal Statements comes from Duke University.

Summary of No No's for the personal statement:
1. Do not give the essay a title
2. Do not use quotations
3. Do not use dialogue
4. Do not write in the third person
5. Do not use the passive voice
6. Do not make the essay a narrative version of your résumé
7. Do not use footnotes
8. Do not tell them about the law, talk about you
9. Do not be repetitive
10. Do not read one of those "Winning Essays That Got Me into Law School" books
11. Do not compare yourself to other people, i.e. "I may not be as smart as many of your applicants, but I study hard." or "While my classmates are out partying, I am in the library working hard!"

Fortunately, Duke also advises on what you should include. Top schools want students who have excellent potential. They want to produce lawyers who will make them proud by achieving success in their careers. Put your heart into this letter because it could be the thing that moves your application to the approved stack.

There have been isolated instances when applicants have asked someone else to write their personal statement. This is pure lunacy and for the clear majority of my readers even mentioning this strategy is an insult. But somewhere out there someone is paying someone else to write their letter because they think it will increase their odds of getting into a program. If you aren't smart enough to write a letter describing your own reasons why you want to study law, you have no place in a law school or the legal industry.

If you need help, there are legitimate career consultants who can assist with every step of the process. These individuals often come out of academia and have inside knowledge of what schools are looking for. From an organizational aspect, they can be a tremendous asset because they have constant interaction with the law schools. By learning about you, your academic history, and your future goals, these consultants can help you perfect your application package and find the best opportunities for you. These services aren't free but could be meaningful to applicants who don't know where to start or who might need a guiding hand.

If your LSAT score and written statement are good, you might have to take one more step. Some law schools will want to meet prospective students before admitting them into the program. These meetings may be conducted on the phone, video conference or in person. The University of Chicago handles interviews via Skype, even for candidates who live in the Chicago area. If you get this opportunity be excited about it. Don't try to over-prepare for it. Be yourself, be honest about what you want from the program and what you think you can contribute.

Acceptance is only part of the consideration. You should also recognize not all law schools are good schools. Even some of the accredited schools are not great, and odds are you may be very disappointed with the results if you attend. In the world of jaded law students, bad law schools have the shameful distinction of TTT or Triple T, which stands for Third Tier Toilet. If you search this term on the internet prepare to see the worst, written by those jaded folks I warned you about earlier. Significant hyperbole surrounds poorly performing law schools and most of the complaints are voiced by those who attended and are bitterly disappointed with their personal results and failures. While some of these schools deserve their poor reputations, disgruntled alumni amplify the discordance. Don't buy into the vitriol. Research, rankings, references, and bar pass rates are much safer metrics to measure your school. I find it interesting that people who have to resort to attending the lowest ranked schools somehow expect a better experience for their own education. There is a clear reason why the lowest schools are ranked where they are. They have earned the distinction. Don't worry though. With a good plan in place, you can find the right school.

7

Law School and Clerkships

I'm not going to spend too much time discussing survival techniques for law school. There are books and blogs written about how to master your law school experience, but your real life encounters are going to help more than anything. As soon as you become a first-year law student, or a 1L, you are going to meet many 2L and 3L students and they will tell you what they have experienced in your specific program. I'll offer a summarized view just to challenge or validate some of the commonly held views. Once you are in the program my best advice is to simply hold on and keep moving forward. Getting into a good program is a major accomplishment, so don't screw it up!

Try to start the program as strong as you can. You get a fresh start on your grades because from this point on most people will only focus on your law school marks. GPA matters in law school, even more than it did in your undergrad program. Your law school GPA has the potential either to help or hurt your employment prospects for years to come. Some firms have very high standards when it comes to clerkship or entry-level Associate offers. If your grades are low, you won't get a shot even to speak with some firms. It's similar for your class ranking. Many firms will only consider the top 10% or 20% of a class for clerkship consideration. It doesn't stop there though. I've worked with high-end firms seeking a sixth-year lateral Associate and they still wanted to see transcripts to ensure they were only hiring top performers.

Clearly your focus should be on your course work, but you should also meet everyone you can. Join the ABA as a student member. Seek out and join student organizations. There is an organization for students with just about any background or interest. Yale Law school has more than 50 groups focusing on topics related to social and civic issues, ethnic groups, and numerous areas of law. Make friends and start networking. Remember that every person you meet is someone you may encounter numerous times during your career. The legal industry is large but feels much smaller when it comes to your reputation. As a lawyer it will seem like there is always someone who either knows you personally, or they know someone who knows you. Even after a decade of practice you are likely to encounter job opportunities and potential client referrals by someone who knew you from law school. You'll also find your school's alumni network can be a goldmine for the rest of your career. Aspects of the smaller community can work against you as well. If you are an awful student and a jerk in the program, that reputation will follow you beyond graduation.

There is more than one way to earn a Juris Doctorate. Years ago, the vast majority of lawyers earned their law degree in the same manner. They graduated from an undergrad program, applied to law school, got accepted and spent the next three years in a law degree program. The traditional full time JD programs are still the dominant model and almost always require daytime courses over a three-year period. These programs usually require your full-time attention. It's a huge challenge to concurrently maintain a full-time career and attend a full time, traditional three-year JD program. While it might be possible to attempt both, those individuals foolhardy enough to try it might end up with diminished results in both work and school.

Some schools have adopted a four-year part time program with classes occurring in evenings and on weekends, targeted directly at those students who are working full time or have family care issues during the day. There are many who could never attend law school without this option. While it is a legitimate path to earn the same degree, part-time programs have their own challenges with one example being the logistical issues of obtaining a summer clerkship. Some larger firms are so hard wired in their existing process that dealing with a 4L simply doesn't fit into their process. It is a challenge to work and attend law school but if you choose to do so think hard about the time commitments. McKinney Law at Indiana University lays out the expectations: "First year part-time evening classes are five nights a week, Monday through Friday from approximately 5:30-8:30. As a general rule, a student studies 3 hours for every hour they sit in class. Part-time evening students attend class 2 hours each evening and they can count on approximately 6 hours of study for each evening's class." IU McKinney has sometimes been called "the school that never sleeps" and if you work and attempt the JD program you'll understand that motto even better.

A quick word about cheating. I shouldn't even have to address the topic, but I must because it still happens at universities and even in law schools. It's mindboggling but academic dishonesty does occasionally rear its ugly head. If you cheat or if you stand idle while others cheat, please do society a favor and do not bother attempting a career in law. Being kicked out of law school as a cheater will be a stain that is hard to remove. Get caught cheating in law school and you might as well start looking for an entirely different career, even if you manage to survive the ordeal with penalties and strict probation. Your school might spare you, but your classmates will never forget your actions. In this business your reputation is critical, so don't squander it over something stupid. The practice of law is reserved for people of strong character and the courage to stand for what's right even when others will not. Do not bring shame to yourself and others by cheating. If you are even remotely considering it just remember, it's easier to explain a poor GPA than it is to explain why you got kicked out of your school.

If you want to work in a large law firm you really should do a clerkship, preferably two clerkships while you are in school. In the U.S. securing a clerkship can have a profound impact on your future career options. The more options you have, the better. Commonwealth country law students don't have clerkships — they take an articling job. In places such as Canada articling is a mandatory, fixed period clerkship. You spend 10 months working in an apprenticeship that occurs under the tutelage and supervision of an established lawyer. There is another experiential training path for the smaller group of students who can't find an articling job. The educational system itself works hard to ensure that future lawyers get some experience under supervision before they practice.

In the United States there is a similar desire for law students to get experience, but clerkships are not mandatory. You may hear about judicial clerkships or summer clerkships. A judicial clerkship is something you can do after you graduate. These are typically a one or two-year assignment with a court, working directly with a judge. The positions are highly sought after because they give a lawyer an incredible learning experience, literally at the feet of the masters. The positions are so prestigious that many firms make a law graduate, accepted into a judicial clerkship, a job offer for the future to begin after their judicial clerkship is complete.

For our purposes I'll focus on summer clerkships, the very common programs that many students do over the summer while in school. Obtaining a clerkship is highly recommended to increase your odds of a job offer before you graduate. American legal clerkships are usually eight to ten-week summer programs. Those which occur in private practices are usually packed with an abundance of social activities and time to meet the attorneys at the firm. It's an opportunity to experience the firm's culture and work environment first hand. In a sense the clerkship is part interview, part audition, part skills assessment, and part social testing. At the end of the clerkship, it is very likely that several people in your clerkship class will receive offers for employment after graduation. It's serious stuff.

Securing a clerkship will take proactive effort on your part. As a law student you'll be focused on your studies, which means making time simultaneously to study and prepare for your career is difficult and definitely stressful. Fortunately, you have help on your side. In the early 1970s the National Association of Legal Placement (NALP) was formed with a mission to enhance the way the legal community recruits and develops professionals for the industry. During its lifetime NALP has worked closely with law students, law firms, and law schools to create a standardized law clerk recruitment process. Most law schools and law firms voluntarily embrace the NALP process.

While you can independently secure a clerkship at a firm, it's much easier to go through your school's formal program to reach many firms at once. NALP helps law schools and law firms work together to set up a system for interviewing students for summer clerkship programs. While it's possible to get a clerkship during your first year of school (1L) many clerkship programs focus on second year (2L) students. They do this because it allows them to see more of your grades. The timing is also right for recruiting. By clerking at the end of your second year of school, you are also more likely to accept a job offer for a position which will begin right after graduation.

Your law school will provide you all the information you need to get started. At certain times of the year they will host on-campus interviews (OCI) and numerous firms will come out to campus to interview potential clerks. There may be a limit on the number of firms you can meet, or you may have to bid on a set number of firms for interviews. Most likely your law school has done a good job securing numerous law firms who are interested in finding talent at your school.

You can learn everything you could possibly need about OCI on the NALP website. NALP is a goldmine of information because they require participating firms to provide a great deal of data about their firm to participate in the program. Firms who interview on campus fill out a form which details their hours requirements, starting pay, and other expectations. Be warned though, sometimes the information can change.

Clerkships are critical if you want a job at a larger, international law firm. Many larger firms only hire first year lawyers through these programs. They want to hire through their clerkship program because it's a system they are comfortable with. Walking into a first-year Associate job at a large law firm without clerking is almost impossible. The bigger firms are deeply invested in their programs.

During a clerkship you'll spend 8 to 10 weeks working at a firm, doing legal research and getting to know the firm and its lawyers. Many programs contain non-stop social outings. While it seems like a really fun work assignment, the entire system should be viewed as a long working job interview. Law firms use the time to identify and confirm the preferred attributes of their potential hires. They want to see that you can do good research, write reasonably well, and get along with people in their environment. Any one of those can be a deal breaker. I've seen clerks who were loved by everyone get passed over because their writing skills were atrocious. I've also seen people who were viewed as gifted writers get passed over because they were painfully awkward socially, or, worse yet, they were a huge jerk.

Investing in a new hire is a big commitment, not just in salary but also in time and effort. The clerkship is a test run for law firms. It not only helps firms identify the talent they want, it helps them identify the talent they don't want. Hiring the wrong person creates numerous problems and can be a major distraction. While you won't see it, behind the scenes the firm is reviewing your work product and surveying the people you are working with. Your performance and your attitude are being measured. You'll be a topic of conversation at firm recruiting meetings.

Some have criticized summer clerkship programs as a bait and switch ruse because of the emphasis on so many social opportunities. During your clerkship you may be treated like a

VIP. You may clerk at a firm that will wine and dine you during your time with them. Someone may take you out to lunch or happy hours several times a week, or even daily. You may be invited to dinner with senior Partners at the firm. If they like you, they may increase their efforts to win you over. Just don't expect that level of engagement once you start as an Associate.

If you get a clerkship work your butt off. Arrive early, stay late. Be flexible and eager to help. Accept any project you are handed and seek feedback on your work product. While you are there you will get a feeling of the firm culture — although the fun and comradery may be overstated a bit. Even if you don't think the firm is the best long-term fit for you, do everything you can to secure an offer. The more options you have the better. By the time you graduate some of the people you have met will have already moved on to other firms. It's good to have contacts at multiple firms.

Most people will take full advantage of the clerkship opportunity and gain valuable experience. Others will get a bit too carried away with the regular socializing. There is no shortage of stories about law students who blew their clerkship. Clerkships often have numerous social events to attend, such as dinners, happy hours, parties, and sporting events. At most alcohol is served. In hotter climates, poorly planned social events in the heat of a late summer afternoon may lead to more drinking by thirsty clerks, and bad decisions by drunk ones. Social events deliberately force people to let their guards down. The firm wants to see the real person, not just a choreographed job applicant. Unfortunately, there are traps laid out and no shortage of people who stumble into them. Alcohol has been behind some terrible scenarios for clerks, including:

- Law clerk gets intoxicated and says something embarrassing
- Law clerk gets intoxicated and does something embarrassing
- Law clerk gets intoxicated and attempts to drive home
- Law clerk gets intoxicated and attempts to drive someone else home
- Law clerk gets intoxicated and partially disrobes
- Law clerk gets intoxicated and partially disrobes someone else
- Law clerk gets intoxicated and makes sexual advances on someone
- Law clerk gets intoxicated and makes disparaging political comments
- Law clerk gets intoxicated and vomits at the event
- Law clerk gets intoxicated and vomits *on someone* at the event.

I wish I was making these up. Unfortunately, none of these are fictitious examples, all these things have actually happened. It goes without saying that very few of the offenders from the list above received a job offer. It's a dirty secret that most clerkship program coordinators know. For firms with large clerkship classes it's not unheard of for staffers to make predictions on which person in the current program will screw it up by treating the opportunity like a party instead of the incredible career opportunity that it is.

The presence of alcohol has been reduced somewhat as the industry has become more aware of the growing issue of alcoholism and drug abuse among lawyers. Yet most clerkships either officially or unofficially have alcohol at their events. It can be a challenge to avoid alcohol entirely. Clerkship program coordinators must plan a variety of events to fill up the summer. During your time with the firm you're likely to have events at bars. You might be invited to a tour of a brewery. There certainly aren't penalties for people who do not drink alcohol, but if you do partake you'll need to practice moderation to avoid a potentially embarrassing and / or career ending incident. I cannot stress this enough — all of the issues I've listed are deal breakers. If you show bad behavior even once it may be enough for a firm to pass on you as an employee. Worse is the lasting consequence, your reputation will be damaged. While the firm may forgive your errors, the other lawyers you meet won't ever forget your actions. Speaking of mistakes, illegal drugs are another absolute deal breaker. If you are in the habit of doing illegal drugs recreationally you are in the wrong career. A drug conviction is likely to be followed by disbarment.

If you did well during your clerkship the firm may make you an employment offer, which will be contingent on your graduation and eventual bar passage. If you split your summer into clerkships at two different firms, you may two offers. This is a great situation. It's wise to think about the things that motivate you during your clerkship. You need to consider a range of issues before the offers go out, so you'll be prepared if you get an offer. Do you want to work in a specific practice group or in a specific office? You may get an offer without a practice designation. You may get an offer for an office far from your home. Think about these things early and be thoughtful and really consider what your longer term goals are. Odds are any employment offer you receive won't be open-ended, so you will only have a short time to consider your options.

After your clerkship try to stay in contact with everyone you met, including the other clerks. This is a great opportunity even if you aren't going to accept an offer from the firm. Having friends who are Associates at other firms can be tremendously valuable. In this business the more contacts you have in your professional network, the better.

If you didn't land a clerkship don't fret but don't waste any downtime. Make the most of your summer. Find something to do that will either develop your skills or give you something impressive to talk about in your future interviews. Volunteer or find some leadership opportunity that will help highlight your better characteristics and ability to a potential employer. Remember the long haul strategy — everything you do has a cumulative effect.

You'll have to cross quite a few hurdles early in the race, but you'll get through it.

8
The Bar Examination

With law school coming to an end, it's time to focus on the next hurdle — the bar examination. Fail this exam, and you can say good-bye to your career plans. The February 2018 California State Bar results paint a striking picture.

Preliminary statistical analyses from the 2/18 General Bar Exam:
- 4,701 applicants complete the exam
- 1,267 (27%) were first time applicants
- The passing rate for first time applicants was 39%
- 3,434 applicants were repeat applicants
- The passing rate for repeat applicants was 23%

Take a moment to ponder just how terrible those results are. Only 39% of the people taking the test the first time passed. Imagine spending three years of your life immersed in your studies preparing for a career that should last your lifetime. You've paid a fortune to pursue your dream, possibly borrowing tens of thousands of dollars in the process. You may have quit your job, you put everything in your world on hold, you worked your butt off, and read a mountain of books. Everyone you know is expecting you to be a lawyer: your friends, family, co-workers, fellow students, etc. And then you fail. It's brutal.

As a law graduate you might have an Associate job offer lined up contingent upon your successful passing of the bar. In fact, your job at that law firm may even begin as a sort of extension of your clerkship while you study for the bar. Your new firm may pay your salary while you prep for the exam and pay for you to take a bar review course. Your whole professional life is ahead of you and all you have to do at this point is pass one more exam.

Could these terrible rates simply be a California thing due to the existence of so many unaccredited law schools? Perhaps we should look at bar passage statistics from another large state with a huge legal market. What about a state like Texas?

	FIRST TIME EXAMINEES				REPEATERS			
	PASS RATE	Number Took	Number Passed	Number Failed	PASS RATE	Number Took	Number Passed	Number Failed
BAYLOR	87.50%	16	14	2	40.00%	5	2	3
S.M.U.	76.00%	25	19	6	53.85%	26	14	12
S.T.C.L. HOUSTON	70.83%	72	51	21	38.46%	78	30	48
ST. MARY'S	43.18%	44	19	25	33.90%	59	20	39
TEXAS A&M	67.86%	28	19	9	21.43%	28	6	22
TEXAS TECH	66.67%	9	6	3	33.33%	24	8	16
T.S.U.	27.78%	18	5	13	22.81%	57	13	44
U. OF HOUSTON	60.00%	20	12	8	50.00%	30	15	15
U. OF NORTH TEXAS	40.00%	25	10	15	40.91%	22	9	13
U. OF TEXAS	54.55%	11	6	5	50.00%	20	10	10
Sub-Total	60.07%	268	161	107	36.39%	349	127	222
OUT OF STATE	42.24%	116	49	67	28.57%	182	52	130
TBE ATTORNEY	83.47%	121	101	20	25.71%	35	9	26
RULE 13 (3)-(4)	42.55%	47	20	27	25.81%	62	16	46
REINSTATEMENTS	00.00%	0	0	0	00.00%	3	0	3
Sub-Total	59.86%	284	170	114	27.30%	282	77	205
TOTAL	59.96%	552	331	221	32.33%	631	204	427

Total of First Time & Repeaters	1163		
Overall Pass Rate	45.22%	#Passed	535
Overall Fail Rate	54.78%	#Failed	648

Well, things weren't a whole lot better in the Lone Star State. The overall pass rate is still not very comforting. Now to be fair, I've pulled a fast one on you for dramatic effect. In California and Texas, as in most other states, the exam is given twice a year. Most states will offer the exam at the start of the year, either in January or February and again in the summer, usually in July. A couple of smaller states may only hold the bar once a year if the number of test applications isn't sufficient to justify the exam twice.

You may wonder why the summertime exam results are better than the results from the January or February exams. Most people graduate within a standard three year program and take the exam in July. To be fair, the July rates are almost always better. Here are the results from Texas in July 2017. Fortunately, only 28% of the people failed in July 2017. It is important to look at the numbers though.

	FIRST TIME EXAMINEES				REPEATERS			
	PASS RATE	Number Took	Number Passed	Number Failed	PASS RATE	Number Took	Number Passed	Number Failed
BAYLOR	92.92%	113	105	8	66.67%	12	8	4
S.M.U.	85.44%	206	176	30	50.00%	6	3	3
S.T.C.L. HOUSTON	66.32%	193	128	65	59.21%	76	45	31
ST MARY'S	73.72%	156	115	41	58.82%	51	30	21
TEXAS A&M	83.45%	139	116	23	53.12%	32	17	15
TEXAS TECH	87.12%	163	142	21	47.06%	17	8	9
T.S.U.	63.64%	110	70	40	41.54%	65	27	38
U. OF HOUSTON	86.14%	202	174	28	69.57%	23	16	7
U. OF NORTH TEXAS	59.32%	59	35	24	00.00%	0	0	0
U. OF TEXAS	91.60%	238	218	20	77.27%	22	17	5
Sub-Total	81.00%	1579	1279	300	56.25%	304	171	133
OUT OF STATE	73.94%	564	417	147	43.22%	199	86	113
TBE ATTORNEY	78.91%	128	101	27	69.70%	33	23	10
RULE 13 (3)-(4)	43.75%	80	35	45	17.39%	69	12	57
REINSTATEMENTS	00.00%	1	0	1	00.00%	2	0	2
Sub-Total	71.54%	773	553	220	39.93%	303	121	182
TOTAL	77.89%	2352	1832	520	48.11%	607	292	315

Total of First Time & Repeaters		2959			
	Overall Pass Rate	71.78%		#Passed	2124
	Overall Fail Rate	28.22%		#Failed	835

This is why it's imperative to attend a good school. Imagine graduating from a program which taught you very little. You take the bar exam and probably realize about half way through that you are dreadfully unprepared for it. After the exam you get to wait for weeks while the results are tallied only to finally get the eventual message that you failed. You do not meet your state's minimum requirement to practice. In fact, calling yourself a

69

lawyer at this point is against the law. So, you re-focus your energy, study hard, and prepare yourself for a second attempt. And you fail it as well. At that point you'll be scrambling for a Plan B on your career. You'll soon have to let everyone know that the whole law thing didn't work out for you. This is the risk of picking a bad school. It may make the difference between you becoming a successful lawyer or becoming someone who has to explain why you don't practice law even though you have a JD, for the rest of your professional career. And don't forget, as soon as you graduate, it's time to start repaying those loans.

Not all states have the exact same requirements for the bar exam, but most have a similar setup following the Uniform Bar Examination (UBE) protocol and require passage of three basic components: (1) an essay portion; (2) the Multistate Bar Examination (MBE), which consists of multiple choice questions; and (3) the Multistate Performance Test (MPT), which tests certain fundamental skills all lawyers are expected to have mastered. Not all, but most states use the same format. Some states have a section with questions specific to their jurisdiction. A benefit of the UBE is that your score can be transferred to other UBE jurisdictions. Your law school will provide you all the information you need to be prepared to get licensed in your state.

For most of you, you'll do just fine. You will have three years of training to prepare. It's also very common for people to supplement their preparation with additional test preparation from the private sector. There is an entire industry based on preparing you for the bar exam. Two of the biggest providers are BARBRI and Kaplan. There are dozens of other providers. You can select of variety of review packages based on how much time and exposure you think you will need. You can take classes online or in person. You can take a self-paced course or a week-long intensive cram session. You'll have a lot of options to choose from. These bar prep courses claim to increase your odds of passing the bar and most of the people who have taken these courses seem to back up their claims. They also offer other services beyond helping you prep for the exam. Some programs even offer tips on how to land your first job as a lawyer.

If you have gone through a clerkship and have an employment offer, there is a good chance your firm will pay for your review course. If they do, they will probably tell you which course they prefer. Even if you must pay for it yourself, doing a bar review course is a no-brainer. There is really not a good reason to skip this step. At the very least, by completing a prep program you will enter the examination with a bit more confidence knowing that you've done everything possible to prepare. You've just spent years studying and all your efforts are going to rest on the bar examination. The odds are in your favor, so continue to work hard and you'll soon have it behind you.

9
Law Firm Structure and Size.
What's Right for You?

In 1978 the *National Law Journal* launched its inaugural ranking of law firms. The largest firm at the time was Baker Mackenzie. Baker overshadowed its nearest rival with the record-breaking headcount of 434 lawyers. Coming in at second place, Vinson and Elkins registered 272 attorneys. Today those are the numbers you might see at a regional branch office of a larger firm. Forty years later Baker McKenzie boasted over 4,000 lawyers in 77 offices around the world but were no longer the biggest. In 2017 Dentons topped the list as the largest law firm by headcount with more than 7,500 lawyers in 55 countries across the globe.

As the population in the U.S. grows, so does its population of lawyers. In 1980 the ABA reported there were 574,810 lawyers in the entire country, that is approximately 25 lawyers for every 10,000 citizens. In 2018 the number of lawyers grew to more than 1.3 million or 40 lawyers per every 10,000 citizens. The lawyer to citizen ratio has been climbing since the mid-1960s and there is no reason to assume the growth patterns will change.

You already know that the business of law itself is changing with new challenges, but don't feel too bad about the industry or doubt your ability to find success working in it. The legal industry has not fallen into despair. Despite what you might hear about struggles at individual law firms, the industry as a whole still employs hundreds of thousands of people and continues to make plenty of money. In 2017 if your law firm had revenues of one billion dollars you wouldn't rank on the list of the top ten highest revenue grossing firms. In fact, with revenue of only one billion your firm wouldn't even have hit the top 20 list. Thirty-one law firms recorded annual revenue greater than one billion dollars in 2017. Most of those firms reported an increase in revenue from the prior year. There is a staggering amount of money being made in this business.

How much money a firm makes depends on more factors that just their size. In fact, size alone doesn't necessarily guarantee success. Measuring a law firm by headcount won't tell you its revenue. Measuring a firm by revenue won't tell you its profit margin. Even the reported profit margins are suspect, as some firms play games with their equity counts to manipulate their Profit Per Partner (PPP) numbers. I'll explain why they would do that soon.

Law firms range from single office, solo lawyer shops to massive organizations with a global footprint. Some lawyers have very low overhead and charge nominal fees for services. Others have developed an exceptionally well-regarded expertise and sell their services at $1,500 per hour or more. Law firm offices can be found in low-rent commercial strip centers and in the tallest, most prestigious buildings in every central business district in America.

The business model for a private practice law firm is, on its surface, unbelievably simple. Law firms are simply professional service firms which deliver their advice to clients for a fee. Although the economics of pricing, the scope of services, and the delivery models have changed over the years, some features have been very slow to change. As a private practice lawyer, you'll find the basic premise hasn't changed much over the years. You'll spend time working on issues for a client and they'll pay you to do it, or at least you hope they will pay you.

Your firm may be structured as a professional corporation (PC), a limited liability company (LLC), a limited liability partnership (LLP), or a general partnership (GP). There are various regulatory and tax issues at play when firms decide which is the best setup for them. At the Associate level you really won't feel the impact of the structure much. The issues have more impact when you become an owner because there are tax consequences in how you are paid and how the profits are distributed. There are also liability justifications for setting a firm up as an LLP or LLC, however some minor variations exist depending on what state the firm is based in. As an Equity Partner you'll need to pay attention to this structure because it can have a big impact on your personal income. A corporation might pay for many of the expenses that a Partner in an LLP would pay personally and deduct through their own personal taxes, therefore the same base pay at an LLP may not result in the same final dollars in your wallet if you work at a law firm set up as a corporation.

If you go through a clerkship and you have great grades in law school, you might end up working at a firm like Dentons, or another large global law firm. Some of you will love it, some of you will hate it. Is Big Law the way to go? There are pros and cons and both large and small firms. Lawyers tend to exaggerate their own firm's positive aspects while painting less than flattering images of the other firms. Everyone thinks their grass is greener.

There is no wrong answer here because everyone has different values and different goals. As your practice develops, you may need to move to find a different platform for your expertise and your clients. The platform issue is a big motivator for many Partners because they benefit from the power of the herd. If you work for a larger client, you will likely engage in matters that require significant resources to service their needs. Often larger clients need a firm to be able to scale up to a high level of assistance rapidly. A major project may require an army of legal assistance to be deployed. In a smaller shop there are limitations of just how much work you can produce.

Some larger clients can't afford the political risk of giving all their work to a smaller shop. Corporate General Counsels face a great deal of pressure to give their work to larger firms, even if smaller firms can provide a similar level of service at a lower price. The issue is often optics. If a company loses a case despite being represented by a larger firm, they will often accept that the case was unwinnable. If they lose the same case while being represented by a small firm, the GC will have to explain why they didn't choose a brand name firm. Many corporate clients believe that the larger firms are better simply because they are larger.

Some practices have geographic concentrations so depending on your developing area of expertise, you might find more opportunities in certain markets. If you develop a practice in the energy sector you will find more opportunities in a city like Houston. If you lean towards public policy, you might fare better in Washington DC. If you develop an expertise in maritime law, it's unlikely that you'll want to locate your practice in a landlocked state like Kansas.

As the biggest firms continue to grow even larger, some have claimed that the entire legal market has segmented into well-defined tiers, and that the top firms are creating a permanent distance between their level of practice and those below them.

The size and power of American law firms are often judged through their AmLaw rankings. The AmLaw 100 is the official annual ranking of the top law firms as reported by *American Lawyer Magazine*. Some claim the top tier is now actually the AmLaw 50. Others extend the review down to the AmLaw 200. A competing survey goes to 350. There is definitely a distinction between the first hundred and the second hundred, and there is no question about the power at the top. Those firms at the very top of the marketplace are well supplied with cash reserves, they have large institutional clients, they are well diversified, and they have the financial resources to obtain and retain the best talent and the best tools in the industry.

Others disagree about the power of the top and make regular claims that bigger is not better. They do not believe the size of a firm is as important as larger firms claim. Defenders of smaller (or less large) firms claim there is no stratification of the marketplace. They cite revenue growth as proof that the size of a firm does not guarantee its success. They believe that larger firms always carry higher overhead, which means higher prices for clients, so consequently they live in constant threat of collapse. They also claim that large firms are in a sense a pyramid scheme, where firms can only survive if they continue to add more bodies at the base of the pyramid.

There are valid arguments on both sides, and both sides often rely on dubious data points to defend their own systems. For example, the argument that the larger firms are always more profitable is not valid. A mid-size firm with a 50% profit margin can easily put more money in the pockets of the owners than a larger firm with a 5% margin. It's wise to treat many of the proclamations with some skepticism because even experts use something as innocuous as revenue growth as a strong indicator of success. Revenue is not profit. Revenue is merely the money a firm brings in. Profit is the final gain at the end of the year when all the bills are paid. If you have money from revenue left over after the bills are paid, that remainder is your profit. A firm can have a 10% annual revenue growth and the results can be terrible news if the margin is declining from the previous year. Rising revenue and falling profit can be a sign of some significant issues to worry about.

It's worth taking a moment to address some of the pros and cons about the size of the firm you may join. There is no wrong answer on which size is best for you. It all really depends on what type of experience you want or need.

Solo or very small shops do often hire Associates. If you are hired to support a firm with 1 or 2 Partners, you may find yourself doing a lot more than practicing law. In smaller shops you won't find as much administrative support, so you'll have to do whatever is necessary to get through the day. You may be Associate, office manager, paralegal, and secretary. Often these are starter jobs and younger attorneys will move on once they've gathered a few years of experience. If you are one of the team and not just a worker bee, you may share in the bounty and eventually become a Partner. Work life can vary but often smaller shops embrace their freedom. It's ironic at times because smaller shops lack scalability and many solos find it difficult to break away for a basic vacation because someone has to be there to handle client assignments. The work doesn't stop if you have the flu or a wedding to attend across the country.

There are other drawbacks. Your firm might simply need a junior lawyer to do junior work and that's it. If that's the case, it's unlikely that you'll move up much. If they don't have a specialization your skills may stagnate as well. There is a finite limit on revenue and profit at very small firms. These firms typically have low overhead and will handle areas of law which are not profitable for larger firms. You'll never see larger firms handling DUI cases or fighting traffic tickets. Working at an unknown smaller shop can also present challenges when you attempt to move to a larger shop. Unless your firm has an amazing niche service for high-dollar clients, your personal brand may not grow much in a smaller environment.

Opening your own shop right out of law school is a risky proposition. With zero experience you don't have much to offer clients and your risk of committing malpractice is higher that it would be at a firm. If you don't have a job you may want to try to find contract work before you start your own firm.

Boutique firms are sometimes thought to be called boutique because of their smaller size, but the real definition is more about the concentrated focus of their practice and not necessarily the size of their shop. Boutiques generally focus on a limited range of services in a certain practice area. A firm may have very narrow specializations and market segments, such as limiting their work to something as specific as matters related to the financing and development of golf courses. Some may focus solely on the litigation in a specific industry and even to a single practice within that area, such as a firm that handles employment law issues for hospital clients. You'll often find leadership who began their careers at larger firms. Many boutiques were formed by former BigLaw Partners who felt they could get a better deal if they struck out on their own.

When most of your work is focused on one area you can develop some expertise and credibility in the marketplace. The biggest threat to boutiques is the narrow focus itself by lacking the practice diversification that can protect a firm when client conditions change. If the firm is too focused on an area that has some volatility, a downturn in that area can reduce profits or kill the firm all together. I'll look closer at such examples at the end of the book.

Mid-sized firms may surpass 100 lawyers as they attempt to grow to a certain level, hoping to create both security and profitability. They often present themselves as a full service firm, however they usually don't offer all the services that bigger firms can, despite their variety of practice groups. Mid-sized firms reach a level of critical mass which means they are just big enough to do what they want to do, but not so large that they lose the desirable aspects of a smaller, more personal environment. The organizational chart of these firms is small enough for you to know everyone who works there. The "we're a family" philosophy is typically a big selling point for these firms. In fact, the desire to maintain that familial feeling is why some lawyers will never consider leaving a firm of this size to move to a larger firm.

Mid-sized firms usually develop a client base within their own geography, focusing often on small and mid-market businesses. They can retain rate sensitive clients thanks to their lower overhead. The lower rate structure is often a lure for Partners fleeing the ongoing rate increase pressure present at many larger firms. Many mid-sized firms can run into problems if they expand past their theoretical maximum capacity. Management of multiple offices can be a challenge for firms with a limited management team. There can be financial constraints which make important infrastructure investments difficult.

Creating and maintaining a truly diversified mid-sized firm from scratch is hard. It can be difficult to maintain the optimal size. If firms don't grow enough, they can risk losing Partners who need a bigger platform for their clients. They may not develop sufficient profits to retain their top Partners. If the firms grow too much they can lose control of their culture. They can also over-extend themselves with expanded lease space. Many growing firms have felt forced to take additional space to maintain their growth trajectory, only to be overburdened with costly excess space when they lose personnel. Empty offices are a big problem for firms with tight budgets, so managing headcount and space can be a constant challenge. Mid-sized firms who show promise often become a recruiting target of larger firms.

Regional firms are even larger, often having between 200 and 400 attorneys, but have offices concentrated in a limited region. These firms have typically secured a very strong position in a region as a mid-sized firm and grew, following market demand in other regions. They can have very strong positions in a broad area, especially if their firm has grown side by side with a successful regional client. Regional law firms are a dying breed because larger firms are constantly circling them, poaching clients and talent whenever they can. Most firms of this size are actively trying to expand to protect their market share and increase their revenue. Without the deep cash reserves of larger firms, when they hit hard times they are prime merger targets. Many of these firms will try to become a national player through acquisitions.

National firms are solidly in the BigLaw realm. The differences between some national firms can be striking. Some are exceptionally well run, while others are continually challenged. These firms were often regional powerhouses who expanded, at times quickly, with numerous branch offices. They are big enough to support larger corporate clients. They can recruit and retain high level legal talent, often attracting refugees from the largest firms. These firms can have headcounts of 400 or more, with coast to coast offices, or at least a bi-coastal presence. Many are stuck in a grow-or-die model, so they are often on the prowl for laterals with portable business. National firms can grow quickly through acquisitions of smaller firms.

Some of these firms struggle to maintain their position on the national listings. They may try to keep pace with their larger competitors when it comes to lawyer salaries. They often strive to maintain the firm's original culture, but that can be difficult during expansion, and even more so if they are acquiring complete firms, especially older firms with their own strong culture. The distance between their offices can create trouble. If they don't invest enough time and effort into management, issues can arise on the edges of their sphere. National firms can be powerful, but their strength may not be apparent in their smaller branches. Branch office politics can be difficult because lawyers in a very small office may demand equal pay and resources similar to those of the home office, even if local market conditions do not warrant it.

International BigLaw is as big as it gets. These are the largest firms out there. They have offices and clients around the world. Some generate revenue at previously unthinkable levels. Kirkland topped the revenue ranking in 2017 with revenue reported of $3.1 billion. Some argue firms of this size will eventually be too big to manage, but that hasn't slowed their growth. Some just keep getting bigger.

If you are working for a firm ranked in the AMLAW 50 or even the AMLAW 200 you will have many resources at your disposal. Training and work opportunities are typically strong. You may travel to exotic places as you service global clients. You may have the ability to transfer to another office, such as London, Paris, Beijing, or anywhere else in the world. Your pay will be top of the market. If you are in BigLaw there is a reasonable chance that your pay will always keep pace with current market rates. If you are shooting for a paycheck at the top of the market, you most certainly have to go to BigLaw.

There are drawbacks at the biggest firms. Some firms have offices which are known to be sweatshops. It's also harder to stand out. Someone will always bill more hours than you. You may bill 2,300 hours one year and still not be viewed as the hardest worker. You will never know everyone in your firm. At some firms there is a constant churn of Partners, which means your plans for partnership might change dramatically if the senior people you work with suddenly move to another firm. While some people in large law firms feel like a cog in a machine, it is entirely possible to have the same type of close relationships and friendships that you can find in smaller firms. Another perk of the experience is the instant credibility you will receive by virtue of your association at the firm. Once you have a few years under your belt at one of the larger firms, moving to other large firms can be much easier if you are so inclined. Moving to a smaller firm may have compensation challenges, since you are likely paid in the top of the market.

There are no right or wrong options when it comes to finding the best size firm for you. If you don't have a job any of these options will suffice. If you have options, it's best to consider what you can do for the firm, and what it can do for you.

10

Law Firm Merger Mania

Before you sign up with a firm you might want to check out the local merger situation. Your new firm may acquire another firm. Or they may be acquired. While there isn't a lot you can do about that as an Associate, you should take a little time to ensure that the boat you are stepping into can hold water. Not all merger talks produce a successful combination. Some talks end with one party mortally wounded. You certainly don't want to be the last hire for a firm who winds down operations a few months later. Fortunately for you, this is an industry where a lot of people can't keep a secret, so the confidential negotiations may be common knowledge in your local market.

The continued consolidation in the industry has created enormous law firms and they are getting bigger all the time. From your perspective as an Associate, you'll see that the largest firms are always adding new lawyers through clerkship programs and lateral Associate acquisitions. This is not their top priority though. Growing future Partners from scratch is a long, costly process with no guarantees. Firms put significant emphasis on lateral Partner recruitment because the benefits are almost immediate. Poaching talent from your competitors, especially those people with good clients, not only helps your bottom line by expanding your client base, it does considerable damage to your competition. Mergers don't always go well for everyone. Unfortunately, the fate of Associates is usually not at the top of the list of considerations when these deals get hammered out.

Firms continually deploy internal and external recruiters to help identify talent. Once they have a list of targets they simply try to cherry pick individuals from their competitors. Big law firms cut all kinds of deals with successful Partners to persuade them to change teams. Although the candidate may feel like they are the center of attention, the firm may be talking simultaneously to lawyers at a dozen different firms. It's a two-way street. Most Partners who are open to recruitment won't simply join the first firm who approaches them. In the end it becomes a bidding war. The variables are compensation, security, culture, trust, and the offer of strong support from a more impressive platform.

Once a lateral team is onboarded the spotlight and the resources can be switched to the next lateral prospects. Some laterals expect the attention to remain on them after they join. If they don't find the sustainable level of support they were looking for, they might move again within the next year or so. There's a lot of movement in this business.

If hiring a single strong Partner is good, hiring an entire team of Partners must be better. Obtaining an entire firm is the jackpot. At least that is the conventional wisdom of many larger firms. There is a constant battle between the largest law firms as they fight to obtain the top talent. In this industry the easiest way to grow quickly is to acquire another firm entirely. These acquisitions in a specific market can serve numerous strategic purposes, such as growing a bench depth of a practice or acquiring a specific client. If you want to enter a new region, acquiring an existing firm is a very attractive option, but the venture is not without risk.

Entering a new market is not for the inexperienced. The initial wave of hires is extremely important because they will be the foundation of the firm locally. In the past, a firm simply coming to town was enough to draw great talent to its doors. Not anymore, especially in the profitable markets, which are saturated with other firms. Some firms have learned the hard way that the old "build it and they will come" model no longer works in major markets. To obtain the best talent you must make strong commitments at the beginning to provide a certain level of support to the initial Partners. This is often done in the form of an income guarantee. Changing firms for a Partner can be risky, so firms will offer a lot to make the deal happen. The firm will justify these deals to enhance the prospects of the office's future success.

Many firms have launched a new branch office with a dozen or so lawyers and boldly announced predictions that the office will grow to more than 50 lawyers within a year. It's often wishful thinking. If the energy from the initial burst of excitement fades quickly the growth can languish. Some firms with grand expansion plans will start to work on the next target market as soon as the dust settles on their new office. This shifts the attention and resources. New offices are generally given a year or so to justify their existence. After that, if they fail to produce they could either flatline or be shut down altogether. Large firms do not like to admit defeat, but they also will not sustain a branch office if the location is a money loser.

Mergers are euphemistically called combinations, but they should really be called what they are — acquisitions. While there are some true mergers of equals, most of the time it's a larger firm acquiring the smaller firm. Firms usually look to acquire other firms outside of their current home markets. Acquiring another shop makes sense because starting from scratch in a new market is expensive and difficult. Acquiring an active firm, especially one with deep roots and strong presence in the region you want to enter, is a common approach. Most larger firms have grown this way. They are constantly scouring desirable markets for acquisition targets.

If you work in a small or mid-sized shop, chances are a larger firm has checked out your firm, and possibly even reached out to your management to see if they were open to talks. If this occurs you will rarely hear about it as an Associate, at least not through official channels. If you have good leadership at your firm they won't let others know when they're engaging in conversations with other firms. Not initially anyway. The mere confirmation of a firm's openness to dialogue can send very strong signals. Merger discussions will frighten many employees. It can signal to the marketplace that a firm may be weaker than it appears, because many of the firms that are acquired did not agree to do so for the love of the other firm; they did so out of economic necessity. A common view is that stronger firms don't get acquired because they don't need anyone else to succeed. Willingly seeking a larger firm to merge with can be viewed as an admission of serious trouble.

An additional layer of complication occurs when the merger talks are public. If combination negotiations go poorly, the market assumptions can be swift and impactful. There are websites that regularly receive and publish leaked information from large law firms and merger speculations are always a hot topic. There are more reasons not to merge than there are to merge. There can be all sorts of business and legal conflicts, differing approaches on equity compensation, and cultural norms that simply don't match up well. If your firm walks away from merger discussions, it's not necessarily the end of the world. If your firm engages in several consecutive public discussions with larger firms and they all fail, you might be in a really dangerous scenario. Some firms clearly put themselves on the auction block in an attempt to find a suitor. If they speak with several firms unsuccessfully they will appear to be damaged goods. The market can assume there is something terribly wrong.

The danger to you as an Associate is twofold. You may see consequences before and after a merger. The mere thought of a merger is enough to send experienced people running for the doors. Those who have worked in the industry for a long time have seen many of their colleagues at other firms struggle through mergers. If the merger advances, some people will be affected. A common and entirely justifiable fear for lawyers is the ramifications of the old "merge and purge" technique.

When firms merge one of the expected benefits is supposed to be increased profits because of an improved economy of scale. Firms typically merge their teams and resources to cut redundancies and expenses. Personnel cuts almost always occur and often go up the ranks, hitting Associates and Non-Equity Partners. The larger firm acquires the name, footprint, and client base of the smaller firm, but they have no intention of keeping the less profitable aspects of the firm they acquired. You will hear strong proclamations from the leadership of the smaller acquired firm claiming they will preserve their autonomy and maintain their previous firm's culture after the acquisition. Results vary. Some mergers are smooth, but many are very difficult. It depends on your leadership. It's not uncommon to see a steady stream of departures from a newly acquired firm. From the outside you won't necessarily know if those people jumped out or if they were pushed out.

One thing to consider is the age of your leadership. Especially in smaller firms, if your Equity Partner ranks are older, they may be making decisions based on a shorter timeline. Some owners want to cash out their chips while the firm they created still has value. While it would be great to know that their planning for the firm goes beyond their own expected career timeline, you may simply not know their intentions.

Even well-established firms can become targets. During a 7-week period in early 2018, 3 long-standing firms in Texas announced mergers. As a result, 740 lawyers were acquired by out of state firms. A fourth similarly situated firm, with more than 300 attorneys, announced an end to their ongoing merger discussions. Imagine the turmoil in a market where four of the largest local firms are engaged in merger activity.

If two firms are in merger talks and the discussions stall, or worse yet get cut off abruptly, competing firms will view it as a sign that the targeted firm's foundation is shaky. As an Associate you may or may not hear about merger discussions, even if they are occurring right down the hall from you. It's just another reason why you need to pay attention and maintain strong connections with the Partners. If you establish solid relationships with Partners who trust you, odds are they'll keep you informed on a need-to-know basis.

While much of the discussion has been about the risks, there can be huge rewards for firms that merge. Many smaller firms find themselves in sudden unfortunate situations and they need a stronger firm to help them survive. The loss of a key Partner or key client in a firm can have immediate negative consequences. There are many firms who have common cultures and goals. If your firm doesn't have a guaranteed path to the future, a merger might be a life line. As an Associate if your smaller firm is acquired by a larger firm, you might even score higher pay, better resources, more work opportunities and a clearer path to promotion.

This is an area where you don't have a lot of control, so the best thing you can do is to keep your head down while still trying to pay attention. While a merger discussion doesn't mean you should start packing, it's never a bad idea to know where your parachute is located.

11

Your First Job and Potential Paycheck

If you are lucky enough to secure a clerkship, you may have a job offer lined up as graduation nears. If you don't have a clerkship the road is a little bumpier, but a job is out there somewhere. According to NALP, in 2017 the legal job market for new lawyers was showing improvement with 88.6% of law school graduates finding work the first year after graduation. In the survey only 71.8% of the jobs secured required bar passage. That means that almost 30% of the graduates who found jobs either found a position that didn't require a JD, or a job where a JD was helpful but not mandatory. A few law graduates will go straight into a judicial clerkship. Some will continue their studies to gain more expertise and pursue an LLM degree. Others will find professional jobs, and some will struggle to find anything.

If your goal is to be a private practice Partner someday and you don't have a job lined up by the conclusion of your third year of law school, it's time to pick up the pace. Use your schools career center, seek help from professors (especially adjunct professors who may still be employed in private practice), network your butt off, meet recruiters, join associations, and make sure all your friends from law school who landed jobs know that you would be interested in a position at their firm if something ever comes available.

If prospects look thin on the ground, you may have to change your expectations and settle for now. Don't worry, there is no shame in this approach. It is important for you to get work experience if you want to make this a career. If you don't have anything lined up, you can easily find temporary work from one of the many contractors who support law firms. These are often document review assignments. I don't recommend going solo because you have no real experience and doing so might create more problems than being temporarily unemployed. I'm sure I will get some pushback on this point because some solos have been quite successful. Going solo is not the path of least resistance.

Don't embark upon your job search with an inflexible set of conditions. Geographic preference can be a big limitation for some people. If you enter your job search with the insistence of working only in your hometown you will cut yourself off from most of the opportunities out there. It's the same with money. If you refuse to consider positions unless they pay top firm salaries, you may not get an offer.

If you don't have a position lined up, your new job is finding a job. Resist the urge to take the summer off after law school. Sure, take a vacation, you earned it, but do not take an extended round the world tour. It's imperative for you to land a job as soon as you can after law school. The longer you go without a job as a lawyer, the harder it will be to find something. Once you land a job, stay there for more than a year, even if you don't enjoy the work. At the start of your career it is critically important to establish credibility as someone employable and dependable. If you leave after only a few months, it may look like you were fired.

One of the worst things you can do is leave your job in less than a year. It doesn't look good. Anyone can hold on to a position for a year, even people who are terrible at their jobs. Some law firms can be slow to deal with underperforming lawyers. You may get the benefit of the doubt for six months and then it may take your firm another six months to figure out how to get rid of you. You can certainly move firms, but you don't want to make it a yearly habit. Move three or four times before you make Partner and it can come back to haunt you.

Having a trail of jobs does not convey that you are a desirable employee. It tells prospective employers that you are a job hopper. At the entry level this isn't as noticeable, but if you change jobs frequently as an Associate, you'll find it will get harder and harder to find the next job. While there may be completely reasonable explanations for each move, some employers will simply assume you won't stay with them very long either.

That being said, if you are in an environment with unethical lawyers or where discrimination is a problem, it's worth the risk to get out of there. It's not very common to land in that situation, but if you do you should try to get out as soon as possible.

Completing a clerkship can open doors for you. As we mentioned earlier, you may secure multiple job offers if you completed clerkships with more than one firm. If so, you'll want to look at more than just the base salary they are offering. Consider the strength of the firm, the breadth of their practice, and the quality of the people with whom you'll spend many hours working. At this point of your career it's all about gaining experience. Go to the firm that will give you the best access to talented lawyers you can learn from. That may not be so easy to determine, but that is your goal.

If you only have one offer, take it. Don't try to be cute with negotiation tactics. Most firms have a set package for first year lawyers and you are probably not special enough for them to make an exception for you. Be happy that you have an offer. If you decline the offer another Associate will snatch it up in a heartbeat. Turn a firm down after a clerkship and you may become a ghost to them instantly.

You may find work at a smaller firm which has a modest pay structure. While we all want to make more money, don't obsess on pay. You will make a lot more money down the road. Even if your current salary is less than you hoped, you are gaining experience and that can open other more lucrative doors for you later. Not everyone will start with the pay offered at an international law firm. If that is your goal you can achieve it later, even from this starting point.

If you land a job at a big law firm you may be placed into a stair-stepped compensation system. You will know your base salary and you'll likely have an opportunity for a bonus. Some firms give discretionary bonuses, others have bonuses based on some subjective measurement, or simply firm profitability. I've seen year-end bonuses ranging from $500 to 6 figures. The range depends on where you work and how things are going. Most firms try to reward their best performers. They do so not only to reward your efforts, they do it to retain you. After all, they know it's hard for someone like you to walk away from a job which has a really good track record of paying big bonuses.

The larger the law firm, the more likely your salary will be set by the pay scales of other competing firms. Law firms don't like losing their best talent over a few thousand dollars, so base pay has been edging up for years as they compete with other firms. The law firm Cravath has been a frequent first mover when it comes to raising industry wide starting salaries, so you may hear about a firm compensating on the Cravath Scale. This is simply a set range of pay based on your graduating class year. Don't get excited about the numbers below. Some larger firms delay adoption or refuse to adopt every salary increase that comes down the pipe. Don't forget that a firm has to make money off your efforts, so you'll be working hard to earn that impressive paycheck.

Class Year	Starting Compensation
1st Year	$190,000
2nd Year	$200,000
3rd Year	$220,000
4th Year	$255,000
5th Year	$280,000
6th Year	$305,000
7th Year	$325,000
8th Year	$340,000

Why does it stop at year 8? Year 8 is the end of the line at many firms. I'll explain the importance of that soon.

There are a few things to consider about the Cravath scale. As pay levels have increased firms have tried to adjust their systems to minimize the impact on their own profitability. Firms who feel compelled to increase salaries may also raise your billable hours expectations at the same time.

Before you start spending all that BigLaw money, take a deeper look at the average compensation package for lawyers in the U.S. Money is not the number one motivator for all people when they consider job offers, but it's almost always in the top two. Usually one of the first questions I am asked by prospective law students is about pay, so let's dive into that topic.

In 2017 NALP reported the overall median first year salary in private sector firms as $135,000. About a quarter of first years made less than $115,000. Private practice lawyers make a lot more money than public sector lawyers, so when you look at the average salary for all lawyers the average pay level drops. According to the NALP surveys, the median entry-level salary for an attorney in the public sector was only $48,000.

I've given many presentations to pre-law and law students and I generally review average salary data, often to the utter shock of my audience. I explain that a City Attorney or Municipal Prosecutor might make only $45K to $55K, which is less than one might make as a secretary in a larger firm. Here's a list of positions from a major city in Texas, posted on February 2018 on a website for local governments. You can see the salary progression for lawyers in this particular municipality.

Assistant City Attorney I: Starting salary $57,377.06
Assistant City Attorney II: Starting salary $63,115.00
Assistant City Attorney III: Starting salary $84,005.22
Assistant City Attorney IV: Starting salary $92,407.12

Does a City Attorney IV position really only make half the starting pay of a first-year attorney at a big law firm? Can that be right? It is, in the bigger cities. But of course, a first-year attorney is not eligible for that job anyway. That particular position City Attorney IV position had a minimum requirement of 15 years of increasingly responsible experience as a practicing attorney.

You will be happier in law if you enter the profession with reasonable expectations. Would you pay $150,000 for school to get a job that pays $50K? Perhaps. After all, it's supposed to be a career that will span a lifetime, right? Many law students approach me after my speeches to tell me they have never been provided detailed salary information. They only hear about starting salaries at the big firms. There's a reason why some programs don't like to highlight salary trends. They don't want to discourage you or other prospective students who may enroll later.

Right now, the biggest law firms are offering first-year lawyers starting salaries of $180,000 to $190,000. You almost always have to work in large firms if you want to make that level of pay at the start of your career. Your results will be influenced by many factors. To land the big salary most people need to graduate from a good school, at the top of their class, and successfully complete a clerkship at a big firm. There will be many other opportunities for you, but if you want the top tier pay you have to start at a top tier firm.

Don't forget about student loan debt because a large percentage of law students borrow money to pay for school. *US News* ranks law programs on a variety of issues including the amount of debt held by graduates at the time of their graduation. In 2013 the average indebtedness of graduates from the Thomas

Jefferson School of Law was $180,665. By 2017 the average debt at Thomas Jefferson had increased to $198,962. 91% of their graduates came out of law school with debt. The top 100 schools listed in the survey all had an average indebtedness from law school greater than $100,000.

So, what do you need to know about the money? You'll be compensated in three different ways. You'll have a base salary. You should have the option to receive a discretionary or formulaic bonus. You'll also receive benefits, some of which are as good as cash.

Compensation and benefits range vary wildly by firm. Some firms are known to share the wealth. Others are known to be a bit greedier. One interesting way to view your firm's compensation philosophy is to research its spread in compensation between its top-paid Equity Partner and its lowest paid Equity Partner. If you work at a large firm the legal media will report these details from time to time. In a lower spread firm, the ratio could be 3 to 1, meaning the top Partner would make no more than $750,000 if the lowest made $250,000. For many firms the ratio is 9 to 1 or 10 to 1. For some firms, it can be higher than 20 to 1!

Of course, we assume that some of these pay ranges are justifiable based on the amazing performance of the Partners at the top. An excessive ratio can be seen as a threat to some younger Partners. Younger equities who bring in a great deal of business don't always receive immediate rewards for their success. If they believe the distribution of the wealth unfairly rewards those at the top, they might decide to seek their fortune at another firm. It's complicated. Changing a firm's equity compensation system is a risky endeavor. It can save a firm, or it can kill a firm.

You can tell a lot about a firm by examining their approach to compensation. Firms pay for what they value. You can inquire about their bonus system and you may find a system that rewards hours billed, or the bonus may be entirely subjective. At times these systems may seem unfair. For example, some firms still pay a bonus based on hours, offering higher bonuses for people who bill more hours than an efficient person like you. A very slow worker might produce more hours, but was the work all legitimate if they spent 20 hours on a project that should have only taken 5 hours? Of course, you shouldn't judge an Associate by their billings or collections since most have almost no control on what assignments they take, what gets billed, or what ultimately gets collected. Yet some firms take all these factors into consideration.

If your section is slow you might get a poor bonus, even if you are willing to work around the clock. You might put in extra time for six months, only to suffer through a drought where you have no work at all to do. Will your bonus consider this? Maybe, maybe not. There are many factors. You'll soon hear stories from your colleagues and perhaps even from management. Take everything with a grain of salt.

As you start your career be aware that at some point you will receive an official evaluation. This may or may not actually tie to your compensation. Many firms still maintain an annual evaluation system, and some are entirely worthless. There are a whole host of ugly secrets about evaluations in law firms. For starters, the evaluation process is often inconsistent and at times too subjective, even in a seemingly objective environment. The larger the firm, the more challenging the process. In a firm with hundreds of attorneys and multiple offices, it's impossible to deploy the exact same standard for everyone because of the number of evaluators involved. Not all evaluators will take the exact same approach, nor will they value the same characteristics equally. Each may bring their own sensibilities, interpretations, and unique spin to the process.

Some firms do have a thoughtful system and they can offer truly helpful guidance for your career. You will figure out where your firm stands after your first evaluation meeting. For some firms, the evaluations can simply be rubber stamps. They offer no real road map for success in your career. They can focus too much on whatever happened to you in the month or two before the evaluation. You may be evaluated by someone you've never even met. If you voice a complaint, your candor during these meetings is more likely to hurt you than help you. Goals or aspirations discussed in an evaluation meeting may or may not be followed up with action items. Too few firms set follow-up meetings to discuss the corrections and course changes if you are heading in the wrong direction. Not enough firms develop an actual go-forward plan using the materials from the evaluation.

If you want real feedback, ask your immediate supervisor. Speak to the Partners who provide you with work. Adjusting your career should not be something you do once a year. Be a good employee and play along with their system, but don't take anything as a guarantee of your future success. Track your own progress and discuss it with your boss. If you want to be an owner in the future, you'll have to earn it.

A final thought about your pay. As an Associate you should receive an annual raise. At the bigger firms your pay schedule and increases may occur in lockstep with your peers for seven years. It's very common for lawyers to adjust their standard of living with each consecutive raise. While it's great to get a solid raise every year you are an Associate, there is no guarantee that you'll get regular increases after you have passed the 7th or 8th year mark. It's a big mistake to assume that big annual increases will always occur because at some point you'll transition out of an Associate position and your salary situation may change drastically.

12
Career Paths and the Quest for Equity Status

Finding that first job is a monumental achievement. Most people are so thrilled to get to this stage that they aren't terribly focused on their long-term career plan. That's not a problem right out of the gate. You've endured enough stress so it's not a bad idea to focus on settling in and getting into a comfortable routine. Don't get too comfortable though, because if you want to be an owner of your firm someday, you've got work ahead of you.

At some point when you come up for air you'll start to hear more details about life at your firm, more than anyone ever told you during an interview. You may or may not be assigned a mentor. If you get one, he or she could be great or terrible. You probably won't have much say in the matter. You may have colleagues who are fortunate enough to have amazing mentors, while your own assigned mentor hardly makes time for you. There is a certain randomness to it all that may seem disorganized at first.

At some point you'll hear about your firm's partnership system and inevitably you'll hear about the pathway to promotion. Some firms have a very well-defined path to partnership with clear expectations of your professional skill development, complete with definitions of how and when you'll receive the training necessary to achieve these goals. Or you might end up at a firm with some rather vague and subjective partnership requirements which change year over year depending on how the winds of fortune blow.

The legal industry is somewhat unique in a sense because it hires junior professionals with the belief that one day they will be owners of the business. Here's the hard thing about the partnership track. You'll talk to people who are sure you are on the right path. You'll talk to others who don't think you are. It can be hard to tell who is correct. When I get into the discussion of the traps you'll find out why this is so complicated at many firms.

The partnership track is the period of time and set of requirements that must be accomplished in order to become Partner. This is another area where the rules vary greatly by law firm. Some firms have a very rigid, well defined path that concludes at the end of an Associate's seventh year of practice. Strict firms may believe in an "up or out" philosophy. In those firms, lawyers who fail to meet the requirements of promotions by the seventh or eighth year find themselves without prospects of partnership at the firm. They may be out of consideration for partnership or they may be out of a job altogether.

The 7 to 8-year time frame is not arbitrary. Most firms feel that a lawyer needs 13,000 to 14,000 hours of practical experience before they are ready to operate at a Partner level. Associates are occasionally asked the question: "Are you on the partnership track?" Unfortunately, many times the answers are "I don't know" or "I think so." Working the hours is not all it takes. It is difficult to gauge your progress on the partnership track in a firm with subjective criteria, inexact measurements, poor evaluation mechanisms, or rules that change along the way. Unfortunately, some firms exhibit all of those negative characteristics despite their best intentions to create a fair and easily navigable system.

Each firm is different. For some firms the path can be longer. Some firms are closed shops regardless of what they say they are.

This occurs more often with smaller firms. In these firms a limited number of equities, or even a single owner, restricts the equity stake and has no intention of ever opening up the equity ranks to others. They want the entire profit pie for themselves, and even if they are generous with pay, benefits or bonus, they have no intention of sharing the profits. Closely held partnerships, like closely held private companies, don't have to report their numbers and feel no obligation to be transparent in their finances or decisions.

For most lawyers their first promotion to Partner, Shareholder, or Member does not give them an equity stake. You may wonder why firms don't just make everyone an owner after they've put in enough time. Money isn't the only reason, although it is the main reason. Most firms have tiers of partnership. In firms with a multi-tiered partnership, your first promotion will probably be to a Non-Equity Partner position. These positions can also be referred to as income partners or special partners. The equity status is typically not disclosed to the outside world. As a Non-Equity you may have the exact same external title as an Equity Partner, you just won't have their perks or a stake in the business. I'll discuss more details of this status deeper later in the book.

I'll assume for a moment that you're going to get promoted. The chart below shows typical pathways from clerkship to Equity Partner. You'll notice that a lot of folks don't start on the first rung of the ladder — they lateral in later. The number of lawyers who stay at one firm from law school clerkships to Equity Partner is a number that grows smaller every year. Most firms grow through lateral acquisitions. Training a first-year lawyer has its risks. Firms invest considerable time and resources into the training and development of a young lawyer. Some invest less than others, but the compensation alone makes the hiring of a first-year lawyer an expensive endeavor, especially since there is no guarantee the lawyer will stick around long enough to become a Partner.

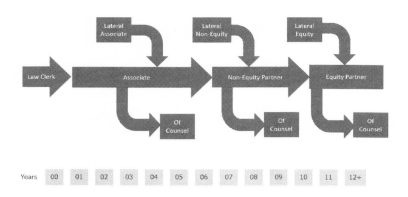

You'll notice that some people leave the partnership path to become Of Counsel. This overused title means different things at different firms. The ABA has weighed in on the topic over the years. If you are Of Counsel it basically means you have a working relationship with the firm, but you may not fit neatly into their existing titles or org chart. You might work a little or you might work a lot. Anyone can be Of Counsel. Senior Associates who don't get promoted might be given an Of Counsel title because the Associate title is no longer suitable for their level of experience. Non-Equities who don't make it to Equity may become Of Counsel and engage in other, non-conflicting pursuits. Even Equity Partners can scale back, sometimes surrendering their equity status to adopt the Of Counsel title. The title doesn't matter if you're off the partnership track. They have to call you something; Of Counsel, Senior

Counsel, Senior Attorney, whatever. The choice of a title can be quite political, and many lawyers will hang on to the Of Counsel title even if they rarely practice. Law firms don't really care as long as the individual's compensation correlates fairly to the level of contribution they make.

Why so many laterals? You will see this immediately in your career. Lawyers move around frequently. Associates usually quit for stronger opportunities elsewhere, either more money or a better shot at promotion. Often, they make moves around year 6 or 7 when they give serious consideration to the rest of their life. It's not uncommon for Senior Associates to leave private practice for an in-house position at a corporate legal department around the time they should be considered for promotion. I'll discuss that in more detail later. Non-Equities may leave for more money, but often they leave because they aren't happy with the plateau they have encountered at their firm. If promotion seems unlikely they may try to find a better deal elsewhere.

You'll hear a variety of explanations on why people at your firm leave. Departing Equity Partners almost always leave for better compensation, or at least the potential of more money. Many Equity Partners demand a certain level of comp, even though they know that a firm's profit can rise and fall over time. If their pay drops below a certain point they will consider their options. If things seem uncertain at their firm, some may bail to save their own skin. It's not a hard thing to do because there are so many opportunities out there. If an Equity Partner has a big book of business, they will always have options. Since there is a certain presumption of success at this level, other firms are always eager to talk to lateral Partners.

As an Associate it is wise to consider your own timeline plan going forward. I'll review a sample plan in the following chapters. Your plan may vary, especially if you take time off to have a child. In the past parental leave used to pause advancement on the partnership track, but it's no longer an issue at most larger firms. Larger firms recognize that retention is improved when they actually allow you time to care for your family.

Regardless of your exact timeline, start to develop your own plan and track your progress. Be aware that any moves or major job changes can impact your timeline. Keep a file with all your important data: hours reports, evaluations, training attended, etc. Ideally, by the time you are up for promotion, you will be able to present a well-documented packet with many justifications for your advancement to Partner.

13

Laying the Foundation of Your Career

Experience matters. At the start of your career you need to throw yourself into your work, observing and absorbing every bit of knowledge possible. The more hours you work, the more aspects of the law you can learn. Early on you may feel that your relationship with your firm is one sided; that you give more than you receive. In reality at this stage the hard work you do isn't simply to make your firm more money, although that is certainly a byproduct of high hours. The time you work is an investment in your own future. You are contributing to your own success.

Law is a business where wisdom and expertise accumulate quickly. It's also possible for your skillset to stagnate if you don't put in the effort. Every experience you have, every task you complete, can add to your professional repertoire. Successful lawyers have a hunger for greater challenges and more responsibility in their work. Once you start at a firm your focus should be on getting increasingly challenging assignments. The experience you earn is what will propel your future career. Some people assume that their years on the timeclock will be sufficient to create a lifetime of opportunities. Showing up to work is not enough. There is not a guaranteed correlation between the duration of your employment and the experience you gain. You may be a fifth year Associate at your firm, but that won't really matter if you only have the skills and experience level of a second or third year lawyer.

When law firms seek lateral Associate candidates they typically start by looking at two things. The first aspect they look at is experience. If you are coming from a strong firm you may get the benefit of credibility based on the firm's reputation. If you come from a small, unknown firm, you may have to work harder as you try to convince people of the value of your prior experiences. If you have five years at a good firm you may be able to get interviews easily, but if interviewers feel you lack the expected level of experience, you probably won't get a job offer. If you ever intend to lateral over to another firm you will have to convince them that you have the requisite experience for the position you seek. If you are a litigator they are going to want to know how many trials you've done. If you are a transaction lawyer they'll want to hear about the biggest deal you've managed. If you work in a specialty area they'll want concrete examples of your experience. You'll need to show that you can handle higher level work on your own.

The other aspect for Associate hiring is stability. If you can't hold a job anywhere else for very long, many firms won't even bother talking to you for fear that you won't last long with them either. No one wants to hire a job hopper.

Law firms will expect you to have a certain level of experience at every phase of your career. If your professional growth stagnates at a lower level it will be hard to advance. You may get a rude awakening if you move to a firm with higher standards. No one at your current firm will tell you how your skills compare to Associates at other firms. You'll have to ask your similarly situated friends at other firms about the types of tasks and assignments they are working on if you want to get a better idea of where you stand. If you are lucky enough to have a good mentor, you will have someone who can direct you and offer advice. Not everyone is that lucky.

Your career will follow a certain path regardless of the type of firm you join. There are some fundamental similarities irrespective of the size of the organization. At the start of your legal career your goal is to justify your existence through hard work. At the same time, you must soak up as much knowledge as possible. You'll start by handling any grunt work you can find and move up to more sophisticated projects as you establish credibility and develop your reputation. Think of the required steps as a sort of modified Maslow's Hierarchy of Needs for partnership. Instead of finding self-actualization at the top of the pyramid, you'll find greater potential for promotion.

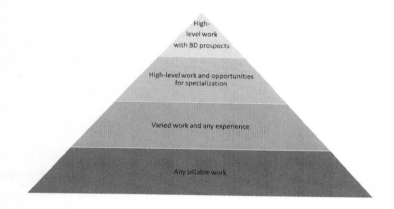

Stage One: At the bottom of the ladder, the first stage is all about finding work — any work. Having nothing to do is dangerous because the firm expects your productivity to cover your costs. You must create value for the firm to keep your job. You must master this level before you can advance to the next step so don't ever turn down a work assignment if you have capacity. Seek honest feedback on the work you complete. If you develop a regular pipeline of projects be sure to keep your supervisors appraised of your availability. If your current project will be completed by the end of the week you should let your boss know your status as early as possible, and not at 4:45 on a Friday afternoon. To avoid gaps in your productivity, it's smart to line up your next project before your current project concludes.

Stage Two: Once you become known as someone who will take assignments and complete them reasonably well, you should seek out opportunities to work with a variety of Partners. You're probably still at the point where you wouldn't refuse any assignment, but as your credibility and connection grows so will your opportunities to ask for higher level work. Some younger lawyers get stuck into a routine as a service lawyer, handling the same type of project from the same Partner repeatedly. Don't panic if it feels like you are getting stuck into a rut. Try to gain as broad as exposure as possible. You need to ask for it. Seek opportunities even if they require a bit of sacrifice. For example, if you need more courtroom exposure, request to accompany Partners who have a hearing at the courthouse, even if your time isn't being billed. Your goal now is to learn as much as you can. Many of your peers will be content with the workload they are handed. Let your supervisor know when you can handle more. Be sure to tell them you're interested in increasingly challenging work.

Stage Three: By this point you have proven yourself as a dependable worker. Once you earn trust from others you will likely encounter opportunities which will allow you to dig even deeper into the areas of law you enjoy. Pay attention, because not all these opportunities will be obvious. At times they are presented in a manner which require a bit of initiative to fully engage. Don't expect Partners to bend over backwards to get your attention. Getting more experience at this phase in a single area can help develop a specialization. Even if you don't get to develop a specialization you should always pursue higher level work. Ideally your projects will get you even closer to the Partners you work with. If they trust you, they'll teach you. Your goal is to learn from the masters and develop a higher level of expertise. Like a new surgeon who gains credibility by learning a litany of procedures, you can learn to handle a variety of functions and earn a reputation as a strong asset for your section.

Stage Four: You're now quite skilled and can run with matters on your own, without constant oversight of a Partner. Now is the time where you can showcase your ownership of a matter. A Partner is unlikely to hand you a client at the start of this stage, but they certainly may give you higher levels of responsibility on a case or a transaction. They may even give you complete control over a smaller matter or a case. If you keep growing and your Partners recognize your career development, you may be presented to a client as part of the team. Having your profile included in a client pitch is a great sign of your progress. Closer access to a client may follow, which may give you an opportunity to develop your own relationships with individuals there. When you get to the point where the client calls you instead of the Partner, you'll be in great shape. To be a Partner in most larger firms, you need to hit stage four by your sixth or seventh year of your practice.

Part of the training you will receive is mandated. Your state bar will require you to complete a certain number of hours of continuing legal education (CLE) every year to maintain your license. The amount varies. In Texas it is 15 hours each year, in Illinois its 30 hours every two years. California requires 25 hours every three years. There used to be a robust CLE industry back in the days when people attended training in person, sometimes at a vacation destination or resort. Now you can take classes online, which is what most people do. Your local bar association will likely present some great options, so don't just rubber stamp the requirement with some generic online class. Find a topic that aligns with your practice goals.

Your firm may have a complete training program for you, or they may not. Larger firms usually have in house training facilities and trainers. You may have technical training opportunities on tools like litigation software. Your firm may provide a stipend or reimbursement for any outside training you complete on your own. Be sure to take advantage of it and track all your efforts. If you receive any negative feedback on any aspect, such as your writing skills, make an investment of your own time and money if necessary to take additional classes. Long term you will not regret investing in yourself.

If you develop a concentration in a certain area you may want to pursue board certification. Board certification shows your expertise in a specific practice area. You can go through a state sponsored program, or through an ABA-accredited national certification program. Receiving a certification usually requires completing a certain amount of training hours and the passing of an examination. Earning this designation is a lot of work, but the credential will be a strong asset for your entire career.

There is one building block you cannot avoid. If you work in private practice the billable hour will likely dominate your life for years. The heavy workload requirement is one of the biggest issues that throws new lawyers for a loop. If you thought law school was hard get ready, you haven't seen anything yet. In law school if you didn't work hard you might get a bad grade. In the practice of law if you don't work hard you might lose your job. Handle a project with less than the necessary effort and you might commit malpractice, endangering your client, your firm and your future career.

The hours component is truly the foundation of your career as an Associate. If you can't consistently meet the hours requirement nothing else will matter. Pace yourself because this is a marathon, not a sprint. At the start of your career no one is expecting you to argue before the Supreme Court. There is a fairly low bar set on the type of work you can handle, which is why your work will often be reviewed by others. Your employer will expect your skill to grow over time. The one thing they expect to see from day one is your dedication and effort. Opinions about you will be influenced by the work ethic you demonstrate. Rather than look at everyday tasks as a burden you should look at them as opportunities to master yet another step in the legal process. All those assignments you'll complete help build your skillset. I can tell you what goes into a closing binder for a major transaction, but you can't really claim expertise until you personally experience the hands-on process yourself. Can you supervise a team working on closing documentation at the end of a 100-million-dollar transaction? That's doubtful if you have not previously mastered the skill yourself.

You're going to have to work a lot of hours if you want to receive financial rewards for your efforts. At this stage you only make the firm money by grinding out work. There are very few shortcuts. You have no choice in the matter. Those who fail to meet the minimum billing requirements will eventually find themselves at risk. Unless they are very successful at client development, Associates who can't hit their hours will be viewed as an underperformer. Law firms don't like paying for underperformance.

Don't forget, this is still a competition in some sense. Compare these two lawyers below, one who hits the minimum budget of 1,800 billable hours a year and another who beats it by 200 hours. After 7 years the second lawyer has 1,400 more hours of experience. Attorney B has likely done more work with more people and may have a leg up when it comes time for promotion considerations.

	1	2	3	4	5	6	7	TOTAL
Lawyer A	1,800	1,800	1,800	1,800	1,800	1,800	1,800	12,600
Lawyer B	2,000	2,000	2,000	2,000	2,000	2,000	2,000	14,000

Most private law firms have a minimum billable hour requirement. What does the minimum really mean? When a firm states a billable minimum budget of 1,900 hours it expects the attorney to record at least 1,900 billable hours per year. That's the minimum, not the goal. Despite the rise of alternate fee arrangements, or AFAs, most firms still rely on the billable hour as a measure of your productivity. It's a terrible metric to measure your success for a variety of reasons, but it may be one of the biggest components you'll be viewed by. There are always stories about how some firms are abandoning the billable hour, either as a way of billing or as a tool to track Associate success. Don't count on that. Despite years of predictions to the contrary, the billable hour is still alive and well.

The NALP forms I mentioned earlier offer details on the minimum billing hour requirements for many law firms. There can be stories behind the numbers that won't be explained in any survey. What the NALP can't tell you is how realistic these reported hour requirements are. There are firms who have a minimum number in place, but the number has nothing to do with reality. If everyone in the firm bills at least 2,300 hours per year, hitting a required 1,900 threshold may be viewed as insufficient. Every firm views and values attorney time in different ways. For example, some firms will count any pro-bono work you perform as time credited to your billable requirement. Others do not, so be sure to inquire before you make major commitments. If you have questions about your firm's stance, ask.

NALP tracks the data better than many of the surveys you may see. The reported average annual Associate billable hours in 2014 was 1,806. Total hours worked were listed as 2,081. These are averages. Some lawyers struggle to fill a day while others pull all-nighters. When you look at a firm's reported averages you should consider some of the factors behind the numbers. Did they count full time equivalents (FTE) or were the averages based on headcount? Did they adjust for the ramp-up period first year lawyers often experience? Did they account for departures, recognizing that most people show decreased productivity before they leave for another firm? Did they adjust for parental or medical leave? 2,081 hours is not heavy lifting. The staff in your firm will work at least 2,080 hours annually because that is the equivalent of a full-time, 40-hour a week job.

Be sure you know the reporting dates the firm is using to track hours — your requirement might be on a calendar year or by a fiscal year or some other specific review period. Be sure to understand the timeline. If you miss your budget you're in trouble. It's important to understand the ramifications of failing to meet the minimum requirement. Do you miss bonus? Could you be negatively affected at raise time? Do you risk discipline? Could you lose your job? All of these are potential risks. Before you join a law firm, it's a good idea to understand the reality of the billable hour at the firm.

The billable hour is only part of the equation. There is also the non-billable part. You don't get to simply go home after billing eight hours. You have to record that time. Every day you'll be faced with many other non-billable administrative tasks, ranging from communications, to training, to client development. At the start of your career you may spend a bit more time on non-billable work as you get your bearings. Efficient use of your staff and other firm resources can really help you keep the non-billable part of your practice under control.

It may seem hard at first, but things will get easier as your skills grow. To help expedite the process, you should embrace anything that expands your knowledge. Attend every training class you can. Volunteer for any work opportunity. Ask questions and seek feedback. Keep moving forward.

14
Law Firm Finances

Law firm financial issues are not terribly complicated but deserve some extra attention. Even if you never aspire to be an owner, it is helpful to understand how the business operates and makes a profit. As a professional service firm, private practices live by the same rules that other businesses must abide by. If a law firm has declining revenue it might eventually suffer in the coming years. If a firm lacks sufficient cash to cover upcoming payroll, it could be out of business in a couple of weeks.

Law firms try to drive profit by cranking out billable work and keeping expenses low. There are only a few levers in the economic machine that really matter. Firms exist to make a profit for the owners, so like any business they must produce more revenue than expense to turn a profit. Revenue is impacted by the amount of work being done, the rates and total fees which are charged for that work, and the success in collecting what is ultimately billed. The profit is impacted by expenses and the leverage of the firm. Expenses in professional service firms can be viewed simply in terms of costs necessary to operate, or overhead. Leverage is the ratio of owners to non-owners and it matters because a larger group of owners requires a broader distribution of profits.

A small tweak to any of these aspects can make a big impact on firm profitability. For example, an investment in technology may produce higher expenses, but those expenditures may be more than offset by much higher efficiency and the additional revenue it helps create. A ten dollar increase in an hourly billing rate might produce higher billing values, but a decline in collection activity might contribute to a decrease in firm profit.

Owners of a law firm can be called Partners, Directors, Members, Shareholders, Stockholders, or any other title they want to bestow upon themselves. The title isn't really the big issue here. What is important is their equity or ownership of a portion of the business, which means they are entitled to a share of the business' profits. Similarly, as owners they are also on the hook for any liabilities, which in a bad situation can create unexpected obligations. This can occur because of a huge disastrous event, or by something as simple as not having enough cash for immediate operational expenses. If a law firm hits a rough patch and fails to collect enough money to pay the bills, it's the Partners who are on the hook.

Everything starts with the time you work. The work you perform for clients becomes part of the firm's value chain the moment you enter your time into the billing system. Your efforts appear first as work in progress (WIP). Your WIP is a continuous gauge of your productivity. WIP provides the starting value of time worked through a very simple calculation: hours worked multiplied by billing rates. You will always carry a certain amount in WIP as your work product goes through your firm's billing system. This time accumulates and should be billed to a client within a month or so after you work it, but it could languish for months before it hits an actual invoice. Your billable time will be combined with everyone else's and eventually presented to the client for payment. Once that time is billed it becomes accounts receivable (AR). Inventory is the lifeblood of the firm, so the total inventory position is watched closely. Your firm will monitor WIP and AR levels continuously.

We mentioned AFAs earlier, but the most common way your time will be billed is through the billable hour, although many have predicted its pending demise for years now. In the billable hour approach the lawyer has a standard hourly billable rate, which is usually determined based on the years of experience or expertise. The more experience you have, the higher your rate may go, although just about every practice has a tolerance level of how high you can bill. Work is typically billed in 1/10-an-hour/6-minute increments. Hourly billing has been criticized for encouraging inefficiencies because revenue increases as the duration of a project expands.

Timing has a big impact on law firm financial issues because everything is focused on a 12 month profit-driven model. Consider the billing timeline. In a perfect scenario, if you work time in May, it will be billed in June and collected in July. The process won't normally move that smoothly. Your partners might be nervously awaiting final payment for that time as the year draws to a close. At year end the profits are calculated and distributed.

It's easy to gum up the works, especially if you fail to enter your time regularly. You might be working for free if you fail to enter your time by the billing deadline. Bills might go out without your efforts recorded on it. One of the easiest ways to offend a client is to try to slip that time in later. No one wants to bill their client for work performed long ago, especially when they have already paid an invoice from that same period. What will the billing Partner do with those late entries? They may write them off — essentially throwing away your time as far as collections are concerned. No time billed means no collections.

Realization is a very common metric which shows the percentage of work completed that is actually billed (billing realization) or more commonly the amount billed that is actually collected (collection realization). If someone simply mentions realization without distinguishing the type, they are probably talking about collections. Your firm will not be paid for all the time you work. You may produce $1,000 in billable value but the Partner managing the client may only bill $800 of your time. Worse yet the client may only pay $500 of the bill. In the example above the billing realization is only 80%. While the client paid 62.5% of the bill they received, they only paid fifty cents on the dollar of the original value. As your time is billed your partners may adjust your billing rates based on client demands. Certain practices are very price sensitive, so it is not uncommon to see rate adjustments in those situations. As an Associate you are unlikely to have much say in the matter. Most firms have firmwide collection realization rates 90% or higher but almost no one has 100%. If your firm has a realization rate under 85% there may be problems with the quality of work being billed, the billing system itself, or even the client base.

You'll notice that rates are often discussed in terms of standard or effective rates. Standard rates are the rack rates you are assigned by your firm. Effective rates are the actual rate values after all the discounts, write downs and write offs occur. Firms put significant effort into determining your billing rates. Associate rates are typically assigned by class year and they increase annually. Firms constantly monitor their markets to ensure that their rates are appropriate. For years the average standard rates of legal work have been increasing. At the same time the collection realization rates have been decreasing.

When clients are signed up they usually sign an engagement agreement stipulating how quickly bills will be paid. Most firms require payment be made within 30 days of receipt of the invoice. Of course, not everyone pays in a timely way. There is a dirty secret about law firm collections. Many Partners do work for clients knowing that they aren't going to get paid or, at least, they know they won't get paid fully and quickly. Yet they keep plugging away at those clients. It sounds crazy, but in some law firms your value is viewed better if you are carrying a lot of inventory. While firms frown upon major write offs from a client, many Partners carry work from numerous clients, so the impact of a single big write off can be offset by the positive collections from other clients.

A few clients out there never intend to pay your firm regardless of how you perform, which is why new clients are often asked to put down a retainer or down payment before work commences. Retainers often don't cover the full amount of time that gets invested. Partners can get stuck in a sunk cost scenario. If a significant amount of time is already invested in a client's project, many firms are hesitant to stop working if the client isn't paying or is paying slowly. They keep operating with the hope of payment. While there are deals set up to be paid at the closing of a transaction or the conclusion of a case, most clients are expected to pay every time they receive an invoice. A Partner can make promises of big payouts by year end, or some other time-frame, and extend their situation. Some Partners can linger for months, or even years, with terrible realization rates. Some firms see through these situations and take immediate action. Others are unsure of the financial impact or they are unwilling to stop work for any client, even if that client has a poor payment history. Firms pay for what they value. If they lack the ability to calculate true profitability for a client or a Partner, they are likely compensating their Partners for productivity because they think they are making the firm money. It's clearly possible to be really busy and unprofitable at the same time.

Imagine a firm that places more emphasis on hours than profitability. In such a firm you could get credit for working hours regardless of whether or not they are ever billed or collected. Smaller law firms often lack the sophistication to determine the true costs of services sold to a client, therefore they have great difficulty determining a particular client's true profitability. It is possible to have a million dollar client who is a drain on firm finances. A client with a million dollars of revenue a year is actually a terrible client to have if the costs to service them is $1.2 million. There are endless examples of firms improving their profit margins by firing a client. I touch on this in the discussion of the "Don't Bill that Time" trap. Often Partners know what a drag their client is on firm profitability, but they keep working with the hope that the situation will improve, or at least not be viewed as problematic by the firm.

As a professional service firm there is no need for extensive facilities, huge investments in materials or equipment, although your firm may pour money into all of these categories. Most mid-size and large law firms have only two-line items on their budget which account for the majority of their expenditures: people and leaseholds. These two categories are typically 80% to 85% of their total annual expenses. It seems so simple, yet it isn't because the dollars can be huge, and the slightest change or mistake can spin everything out of control. The timing of certain issues can make or break a firm. Cash is king in all businesses, and improper management of cash flow can cause huge problems.

Despite the hype around expense and cost controls, if you take payroll out of the equation, expense budgets are easier to manage than revenue. Firms usually feel comfortable with the expense side because the big ticket items are straight line expenses, like payroll or the monthly rent payment. Expenses don't get much attention during the year unless costs spiral out of control or the bottom falls out of the revenue projections.

Many firms beat their expense budget every year, meaning they don't spend as much as they plan. Some firms all but guarantee their success with expenses by budgeting a certain amount of fluff, or cushion, to some line items, essentially budgeting more than they need. This "conservative" budget process provides a safety valve for year end. As the fiscal year comes to a close, if necessary firms can meet various objectives by delaying some payments until the following year. Smaller purchases can be delayed or canceled. The unused funds go straight to the bottom line at the end of the year, providing a nice addition to the firm's profitability.

It's entirely possible to miss your revenue projection and still have an annual profit if you had strong savings on the expense side. In some firms the lack of precision in these fluffy expense budgets masks real spending concerns or vendor management problems which may be occurring. Administrators who help produce year end savings are often rewarded with strong bonuses. While most managers are fair and honest stewards of firm funds, there are clearly some who will manipulate the numbers for their own personal benefit.

You'll hear discussions about overhead and the firm's costs per lawyer or per timekeeper. Firms attempt to measure overhead to ensure that their expenses are under control and in line with their competitors. This is another area where law firms can deploy a creative approach. Some will take the total expenses, less Partner compensation, and divide that number by total lawyer headcount to determine overhead allocation. Other firms will divide the expenses by title, factoring each title at a different value. It really doesn't matter how it's calculated as long as the method is consistent. It's also not the best gauge to measure individuals, since an allocation of direct expense may not be fair to junior timekeepers. Bigger law firms with downtown locations can easily have $200,000 or more in overhead expenses per lawyer, while smaller firms in suburban markets may have half that.

In the event of an economic shock, firms often turn to the expense side and slash expenditures to help them through a tight time. But since most of the money goes to rent and people, the slashing can't move the needle enough unless they are subletting space or reducing headcount. It's often theatrics. Cost cutting is not a sustainable strategy for profitability. Additionally, by cutting important or even highly symbolic expenditures, these actions can actually make things worse. Cutting the regular office birthday celebration may save you $300 on cake and sodas but could cost you thousands of dollars in lost productivity as the staff sit around and complain about how cheap their bosses are. Every decision firms make sends a message, so firms should be very careful handling these decisions. Any over-reaction about financial problems at your firm can reduce confidence and drive the best people into the hands of your competitors. If the market becomes aware of your firm's financial problems, you can be assured the recruiters will ramp up their efforts to recruit people away.

In all likelihood your firm will operate without any major financial difficulties. Problems can occur though. One of the worst indicators of financial stress for a law firm is a "cash call." The cash call requires the owners to personally fund the firm's expenses until the firm has a sufficient level of operating cash. In that situation the Partners aren't getting a paycheck, they are putting their own personal money back into the business. If your firm is ever in a cash call situation you should keep an eye on the top Partners. This can be a very bad sign and some Partners may jump ship rather than grab an oar during stormy weather. The idea of Partners chipping in during a period of slow collections may not seem like a reason to leave a firm, but the situation is usually more complicated than it appears. Most law firms have credit facilities available, such as a line of credit from which they can draw. If they are in a cash call situation it may mean that they are already fully drawn on their credit. It can also mean that they are not meeting a minimum net worth covenant necessary to access additional funds. That can be a huge problem. With so many strong firms out there trying to lure them away, some Partners may not be patient if their firm seems to be struggling with financial issues.

There are many small leaks in law firm profitability which you may not notice. For example, if your firm accepts credit cards, a small percentage of every payment received is lost to cover the processing fees. Firms also run into issues by advancing clients' costs. Many firms will cover expenses for a client, and the carrying costs of those expenses can add up. If a firm is carrying any level of debt while carrying clients' costs, or if their clients have high levels of outstanding receivables, the firm is effectively financing their clients' operations.

Most firms don't have an expense problem, they have a revenue problem. That's why your supervisor should give you a hard time if you fail to enter your billable time by the deadline. Your firm needs the value pipeline full. In addition to monitoring expenses, law firms should be watching the numbers from all angles — by individual attorneys, by each different title, by each separate practice, by offices, and by clients. At the start of your firm's fiscal year you may not notice a great deal of concern about the numbers, but you'll likely notice a heightened sense of awareness as your firm nears the end of the year. At that point people will obsess about final bills, collection projections, and final distributions.

15

The Reports You'll See and Those You Won't

Everything in business can be tracked, measured, and turned into ratios. Your firm's accounting department will produce the standard business financial packets which include income statements, balance sheets, and cash flow reports. Firms also produce a variety of internal reports for management purposes to show everyone's productivity, profitability, and compliance. You may not have access to these, but your supervisor or section head may be watching these reports closely, or not at all. Your peers in another section or office may have proactive management that react as soon as they see someone veer from the expected course. Your section leadership may remain quiet as you miss the expectations month after month, but someone at the firm is watching. If you aren't hitting your numbers, don't take the lack of feedback as proof that your underperformance is okay. Not all firms are great at letting you know their dissatisfaction in real time and some won't say a word until it's too late.

As a new lawyer you'll quickly learn that the billable hour is a very common metric used to measure performance. Your firm will track every hour you work. Your name will be on reports, many of which you will never see. They track your hours every day, as well as the value of your work, what portion of that gets billed, and ultimately the amounts collected from your efforts. Someone at the firm is watching the performance of all the timekeepers so they can measure inventory values and validate their forecasts. Everything is tracked closer than you might imagine. Your firm even knows how hard you are willing to work. They don't just look at snapshots, they analyze the trendlines. They know if you are going to hit or miss budget well before you even know it yourself.

For example, if your annual billing requirement is 1,800 hours, you are expected to bill 150 hours a month. The firm won't wait until year end to review your progress. They watch it throughout the entire year. If you only bill 140 a month for the first two quarters, you will hit the mid-year point with a deficit of 60 hours. That means to merely hit your annual budget you have to bill 160 hours per month for the remaining six months of the year to make up for your shortage. If you have never billed more than 150 hours in a single month, the people who monitor these things will put you on a watch list. If you bill 140 hours again on the seventh month your deficit is now 70 hours, which means you have to bill 164 hours on the remaining months before yearend. While that may seem entirely possible the skeptics in administration are doubting you. They know that the rest of the year will be a challenge. Will you break your performance record for five months in a row? They know your averages and know how many billing days there are in each month. November and December have fewer billing days because of the holidays. December can be a busy month for corporate lawyers trying to close deals before year end, but it can be a slower month for litigators if all the judges on your cases are on vacation. Regardless of the circumstance, it's up to you the hit the hours. Since your effort creates money for the firm you should expect them to pay attention to your stats.

As an Associate you may receive some reports, or you may not. Your firm may invite you to meetings to discuss the numbers, or they may not. Each firm has a different take on what they are willing to share at each level. Pay attention to the transparency because it will tell you a lot about the firm. Are you merely a cog in their machine or are you a future Partner in training? Access to information is important.

Your firm may not share the data it tracks with the Associate group, deciding instead only to share this information with the Partners. If that is the case, it may be difficult to know where you are in comparison to other Associates. Some firms fear that sharing this information will create an unhealthy competition amongst Associates. Associates view these reports with great interest because they invariably rank themselves against others in terms of workload and work ethic. When they see someone lingering with consistently low hours they may wonder why that person is being protected. If they see someone with high hours who doesn't appear to be working hard, they may assume there is some favoritism in the Partner ranks when it comes to handing out assignments. There can be politics behind the numbers, so some firms choose to avoid sharing the reports altogether. Of course, Associates often compare notes, so firms who try to conceal data usually just end up with muddy waters and a great deal of assumption.

If your firm does not share a lot of financial information with Associates you might hear more about your firm's performance from the legal media. Numerous surveys track the performance in the industry and their rankings are viewed as a legitimate record of winners and losers in the legal field. Some firms participate in voluntary surveys which look at every aspect of the firm, down to the penny. They participate because doing so gives them access to aggregate data on similarly situated firms. This data shared amongst survey participants is anonymized and is used to validate everything from a firm's rate structure to their staffing ratios. Many law firms measure themselves against their competitors, and for some firms the practice is an obsession. As an Associate you will rarely see the details, although you may hear about these reports if the firm is trying to justify some initiative or even their own success.

The reports you may see are through the larger legal media outlets. These papers and websites report on the higher-level data points like headcount, revenue, and profit. In addition to the larger surveys like the AmLaw 100, there are many specialty surveys from regional publications, banks, recruiting agencies, and other legal service companies. Law firms provide information to the bigger publications when asked, whether they really want to or not. They feel obligated to participate to ensure the numbers are accurate. Some publications will simply make assumptions on the numbers if a firm doesn't provide details. If you are the only firm refusing to give data on a very popular survey, it can look like you are hiding something. The reports are widely read in the industry and can make a huge impact on the firm. Most of the reports will show year over year progress for all the top firms, maybe even the progress over a three year period.

Rising or falling in a popular ranking is a big deal. The industry can develop a perception of your firm's viability after reviewing just a few simple charts. Lateral Partners and competing firms will monitor surveys to see if your revenue and profit is growing. If things look great you may get more attention from laterals or even firms who want to merge with you. If your trajectory is heading down, you may attract the attention of recruiters and competing firms who will view your declining performance as an invitation to pillage and poach your remaining talent. Perception can be reality and poor numbers can impact recruiting and retention. Lateral Partners with a portable book of business are unlikely to join a firm with declining profits unless perhaps given the security of a guaranteed level of pay. Existing Partners growing impatient with smaller paychecks could depart and take their business to another firm, making a bad situation even worse.

This is precisely why you should not accept publicly reported numbers as gospel. Profit Per Partner (PPP) is a widely-reported metric which shows the total profit divided by the number of Partners in the firm. It's also the biggest bullshit metric in the industry. PPP is viewed as a simple metric to gauge the financial success of a firm compared to other similarly situated firms. It's often manipulated. Although Partners are motivated by yearly profits, they are also encouraged or discouraged by the trajectory of their own earning potential. This is why internal communication is so important. A firm reporting declining profits one year may have completely justifiable reasons for the drop, such as channeling a portion of a particular year's assets into investments that will pay long-term dividends in future years. For example, a firm may have higher expenses as they invest in building a new office to expand into a new market. PPP is often tweaked by changing the equity status of a few people, which alters the overall ratios. There is no public audit of these reports. There have been large firms who reported significant increases in their PPP only to collapse months later.

Profit margin is fairly simple to determine. To calculate a firm's margin, you subtract a firm's total costs from their total revenue, and then divide the difference by total revenue. You always should look beyond the numbers because a snapshot in time doesn't really tell you the complete story. What really matters is the consistency of profit margins over the years and the comfort level the owners have with the money in their pockets.

No single metric is enough to give you the complete picture of a firm's economic health. It helps to also track profit margins against revenue per lawyer (RPL) and expenses on a full time equivalent (FTE) basis. Instead of measuring simply the profit RPL looks at total revenue of a firm divided by the number of FTE attorneys. RPL trendlines over several years can show the relative strength of a firm based on the value of the work it is getting paid to do. One year of data is not enough. A litigation firm that scores a big premium on a major court victory may show an amazing increase one year, but that doesn't guarantee any future performance.

Your individual production numbers will be compared to others. The firm will examine your performance in many ways, including but not limited to your hours worked, hours billed, collections, effective rates, time written off, and non-billable work. Not all metrics are valued equally. This assessment is ongoing and will happen every year of your career. That's why it is important to know your own numbers and pay attention to what is recorded. Mistakes happen from time to time so be diligent and make sure you get credit for everything you do.

16

The Pay at the Top Matters at the Bottom

As a new Associate you may not give a lot of thought to your firm's overall compensation philosophy. Initially, you'll be happy simply to get a paycheck. At some point though you'll want to understand your firm's equity compensation system if you plan to be an owner there. You've got plenty of time to learn the details since you won't be paid under that system for a while. For now, you can learn much about your firm and the business of law by examining how Equity Partners receive their pay. Equities are paid differently than Non-Equities and staff. Even if the firm is a corporation where the Equities receive taxable wages and a W2 statement, the distribution of firm profits can be governed by a complicated system based on firm performance, or individual performance in any number of tracked metrics. Some systems are so difficult that the owners themselves have only a base understanding of how the system works in its entirety, so they put a lot of faith in firm management to handle all the details.

Equity compensation shouldn't directly impact you as an Associate, but it can disrupt your world if your firm takes actions which upset the ownership ranks. If your firm screws up the system or suggests unpopular changes, it could drive some Equity Partners out of the firm. Anytime a good Equity Partner leaves there is a chance it will impact you.

In the meantime, it's not a bad idea to understand one of the most influential issues keeping Partners at your firm. How the owners get paid is extremely important because it locks in their commitment. If another firm wants one of your Partners they will make lucrative offers, some of which your firm may not be able to match. This is precisely why there needs to be more than just money keeping your people together. Even the most dedicated Partners can be swayed. I know Partners who left their law firms after more than 20 years of service. There are many Partners who thought they would never leave their firm only to succumb to an offer that was simply too good to pass up.

Law firms recognize the importance of the issue and often have a standing Compensation Committee. This group helps determine equity compensation levels and manages the firm's equity compensation process. This is not a job for the faint-hearted because the committee's decisions can be controversial. Equity Partner compensation varies from firm to firm and some places have surprisingly complicated formulas to calculate it all. At the simplest level, firms create budgets in a manner to ensure that all their costs are covered. If expenses are lower than expected, or if revenue is higher than expected, or better yet both — the firm makes a profit and the profit goes to the Equity Partners, split up in a manner defined by their system.

Although the systems can be quite complex with many intricate details, in a very basic sense you can think of the Equity payroll as money divided into two buckets. In one bucket is the base pay if the firm simply hits their expected budget. Depending on the structure of the firm, their base might be a regular biweekly paycheck, or it could be a draw on anticipated final pay. As an Equity Partner, the structure of the firm is really important and can have a huge impact on your pay, both in terms of what you get paid and in what expenses you might have to fund personally. If your firm is an LLP you may have to make estimated tax payments on your presumed income. If your firm is a corporation, standard withholding is likely.

The big point here is that if you become an Equity Partner you get a slice of the profit, which means that all of the other Equity Partners have to share a bit of their slice if new Equity Partners are brought on. It's not uncommon for Equity Partners to resist the election of new Equity Partners to avoid the dilution of their own personal profit. That's the bottom line. Not everyone wants to share. To get into the owner's clubhouse you either have to show your firm that they stand to make more money with you as an owner, or somehow lose money if you leave the firm.

Firms can have a purely objective, formulaic compensation system where their pay is calculated based on performance in certain tracked metrics, such as hours, collections, client origination credit, etc. Other systems are subjective, which means the leadership of the firm has discretion to make compensation decisions based on their best judgement. You might think a formulaic system might be more predictable because the rules are so clearly stated, but results vary. A system may give Equity Partners points for seniority, for the size of their business, or any other factor the Partners have agreed on. Their share may change annually, or every other year. They have all likely signed off on an agreement with all the details of their system. Their Compensation Committee manages the system and ensures that the process is fair for all. However, there is always potential for problems.

Objective systems can be gamed. It's not too difficult for individuals to do the math to determine how certain actions might produce greater personal rewards for themselves, actions which may not be in the best interest of the firm. For example, if an Equity Partner knows that his or her percentage of profits is going to change in January, they may play games in December to increase their own compensation. If someone knows their profit distribution percentage is scheduled to decrease at the start of the new year, they may cut amazing year-end discounts to clients to produce greater personal collections before the year concludes. If their percentage of the profits will increase in January, they might actually slow down their personal collection efforts in December and encourage their clients to delay payments until January, earning more for themselves in the next year while doing damage to the current year's firm performance. These games do happen.

Subjective systems may appear less equitable, but if your firm is managed well the outcomes can be quite fair and predictable. Critics of the rigid formula approach prefer the subjective model because it allows them greater flexibility to react to important changes. For example, many comp systems take a multi-year lookback and consider the trendline of performance. They may consider average performance over several years. If a Partner has an amazing success near the end of a period, a firm may want to reward them immediately rather than punt the reward into the next year. Similarly, if someone is responsible for a disastrous outcome, their comp might be adjusted downward quickly, regardless of past success. Subjective systems allow for any number of factors and seek to incentivize people on what they ought to make, not simply on what formulas dictate. Obviously firmwide trust in the system is necessary for this approach to work well.

There is an additional layer to the equity compensation structure. Some comp systems can be open or closed. Open systems operate transparently. The details of the system and discussion are not hidden from view. The Partners can see the details behind the decisions. While that is good, it also can lead to a great deal of politicking. Often the pay level of a Partner will be perfectly acceptable, until it is shown in comparison with others. Most Equity Partners have a sense of their own value to the firm, as well as strong opinions on the value of others. Open systems invite a certain level of critique and the larger the firm becomes, the greater the potential for criticism. A system that welcomes too much participation can become too cumbersome to function properly. Open systems have to be managed closely because the slightest variation from the rulebook can be seen as favoritism.

Closed systems are not open to discussion, so the Partners at large are not a part of the discussions or determination. If the results are not received well, some may complain that the system is unfair, citing the backroom dealings of a star chamber. These systems may seem easier to operate because they are managed by a smaller group, but they require a great deal of trust from the Equity Partner group to be effective.

As an Associate you won't be given much detail by the firm on the content of the current equity compensation discussions, but most Partners won't be too shy when it comes to sharing their opinion on your firm's system. Pay attention to the reaction of the Partners when the budget is approved and at the end of the year when the books are closed, and the profits are distributed. Year-end is an exceptionally busy time in a law firm. While some people are preparing the numbers for the coming year, others are packing a parachute and considering options from competing firms. Few people will walk away from a firm in the fourth quarter if they know they have money coming in December. Some may not be motivated to stick around after those bonus checks are cashed.

17

Law Firm Culture

Imagine being an owner of a law firm with 50 great lawyers. Other firms would love to steal your talent, and they try to do so regularly. In fact, their efforts are relentless. Recruiters reach out to your people daily. In a competitive market, you may not be able to afford the level of pay and benefits of some of those other firms, yet your people don't leave. Why? In a word: culture.

When you ask a lawyer why they like or don't like working at their firm you soon get to a discussion about firm culture. Every firm has its own distinct culture, which is created over the years by the shared struggles and triumphs of those people who built the firm. It starts with the founders. They usually share similar standards and principles, and this creates expectations on how the firm should do business. Firms want to hire and retain people who share their values. Being a "good firm citizen" is a phrase that is often applied to those who understand and act accordingly under a firm's cultural guidelines.

Most employees seek a workplace where they are comfortable with the firm's culture. Money and other perks are powerful influencers, but they aren't enough to retain talented people for the long-term. There are many lawyers who walk away from very lucrative positions simply because they hated the environment where they were working. It doesn't matter what the high level culture is supposed to be, what matters is the practical application in people's everyday work experience. Even the best law firms can have terrible bosses in their midst, and the employees of those firms often depart sooner than expected. Allowing a supervisor to act in contradiction to firm culture is an easy way to lose good people. It has been said that people don't quit jobs, they quit bosses.

People buy into a firm's culture or they are repulsed by it. Those who accept and embrace it do so because they feel like they are investing in a system aligned with their personal beliefs and goals. It's a powerful weapon in business, but the knife is double-edged. Employees can put up with a lot if they support the firm's values. If they feel the firm is taking actions against their own cultural norms, big problems can occur — and not just at the Associate level. Firm leaders are the standard bearers and serve as agents of socialization, although not all are particularly adept at this, or even aware of the influence they wield.

Some firms will view you as an asset with a temporary shelf life, and others will truly view you as part of the family. You will know where your firm stands once you learn the culture. Little things in daily law firm life can either validate or challenge cultural expectations. Gathering in a conference room to celebrate someone's birthday with cake can be a great bonding experience. That same experience can be toxic if everyone finds out that the firm won't reimburse expenses for the staff who bought the cake.

A good sign of a strong culture is the presence of traditions. Ritual is important, and the development of fun traditions can provide a constant reminder of the firm's beliefs. Often these traditions are running jokes, which start early in the firm's formation. One firm had such a humble beginning that the Partners brought makeshift decorations for their lobby during their first holiday season. A Partner brought hunting decoys to mount in the firm's first Christmas tree. Over the years the decoys were always present, even as the firm grew successful.

Their appearance served as a yearly reminder of who they really were.

Most firms make a decent effort. Almost all firms will have holiday luncheons, happy hours, and other special events to create connections. Events which allow lawyers to gather together in a friendly environment without the pressure of the billable hour or client development requirements are much more productive than they appear. These events allow personal connections to develop and grow. They create synergistic opportunities for lawyers to reach out beyond the silos of their own practice. In larger firms there is even more of a need to create opportunities to bring people together. In a very large firm you may not know the names of everyone in your own office. It's always amusing when people chat in an elevator only to be surprised to learn they both work at the same firm. In larger firms, this is complicated by high turnover. Constant arrivals and departures make it hard to track who is who.

You can tell a great deal about a firm by watching how they expend their resources. A good first test is during your orientation and onboarding. At some firms you may spend a day or two filling out forms and attending training on their computer system. You then get shown your office and the work commences. At other firms you may be welcomed with a firm breakfast or luncheon. You may spend an entire week meeting everyone, learning about their practices and a bit about who they are personally. While neither approach is right or wrong, you do get a sense about what the firm values. Introducing a new lawyer to 100 other lawyers in an office is a time-consuming exercise that actually costs the firm money. In a fast growing environment, a firm can have new hires every week, so a stream of constant introductions can be disruptive.

Creating an environment that promotes lasting bonds with your colleagues can be accelerated through deliberate, coordinated leadership efforts. Sometimes a cue from the leaders is enough. Other times an investment of personal time is required. Either way, the return on investment (ROI) is clear. Camaraderie pays for itself in the development of high functioning teams, trust, and shared commitments. Many law firms have realized that working with quality people is a reward unto itself and their culture supports it. Life is too short to work with a bunch of jerks. Accordingly, some firms have adopted policies to ensure that people treat each other decently. With zero attempt at subtlety, these "No Asshole Rules" are a simple reminder of the firm's value. Sadly, not everyone gets it and some lawyers miss out on opportunities because they have a reputation of not being part of the team. The challenge with these policies is their consistent application. A 90% success rate is not good enough and can create resentment and pushback from the 10% who fail to receive the benefits of the policy.

Some people will never embrace the broader culture of their firm. There are many brilliant people who never leave the Associate ranks because they are selfish, awful people. The problem with awful people is that many of them are unaware of how terrible they are. They can linger for a while because there isn't an instant feedback loop. Overly-aggressive, self-preservationists sow seeds of regret which simply take time to germinate fully. If you treat someone poorly they won't forget it. People will remember how you treat them for their entire professional lifetime. They'll also talk about you. These people owe you nothing and will be more than happy to tell others about you, especially if they have great examples of what a colossal putz you really are. If you develop a bad reputation it will haunt you — maybe not at first, but eventually it will have an impact. Your reputation may proceed you if you seek a position at another firm.

If you think you might be a jerk, there are a few simple things you can do to rectify the situation. First, don't be fooled by the money. Don't confuse your paycheck with your personal value to humanity. Your educational opportunities and career choices don't necessarily make you smarter or better than anyone. Don't judge others by your own definition of success. Don't play the "I'm the boss" card. As an Associate you will be superior to the staff on the org chart. That doesn't mean you are a superior person. Managing staff is not as easy as you may think. If you have to tell someone repeatedly that you are their boss, you probably haven't managed the role well.

Exert some effort to recognize and connect with the professionals at all levels. An assistant with 30 years of legal experience probably knows more of the law than you do, and probably will for some time. Their institutional wisdom is a gold mine of policy, procedures, and protocol. If you ask nicely they will share their knowledge. Assume you know everything and you may soon learn the cost of your ignorance. Be open to their advice. Support staff have their fingers on the pulse of the firm and will offer warnings if warranted. You will meet many amazing people on your path. If you connect with them, you'll find the journey to be much more pleasant.

Not all firms get the power of their own culture. Some have been surprisingly tone death and completely out of touch with the needs of their people. One very famous firm had a stellar reputation for the work they produced but the work demands created a sweat shop environment in their New York office. Some loyal Associates at the firm formed an ad hoc committee to investigate and report on the growing concerns of their peers. They prepared a detailed memo and presented it to firm management. The memo itself was extraordinary. The Associates in the office were literally working around the clock and many of their requests were minor. Since they were eating breakfast, lunch and dinner at the firm, some asked for real plates and silverware. Others asked the firm to help coordinate dry-cleaning and shoeshines, so they wouldn't have to leave their desks to handle those errands. In a sense, the Associates were simply asking for better sweat shop conditions.

The firm didn't handle the situation well enough, which was unfortunate. The memo was leaked and eventually it appeared in an article written by *The Financial Times*. This prestigious publication found some of the memo's contents particularly concerning, especially the implications that some Associates might feel obligated to pad their time if they couldn't find enough work. Many of the firm's clients read the article and had similar concerns. Past invoices were audited, clients questioned the legitimacy of their prior payments, and suddenly the firm found itself in very hot water. In the end the firm issued significant refunds and was forced to make drastic adjustments. Had they simply cared enough about creating a strong culture that respected and listened to their employees, they could have avoided a very traumatic and costly situation.

18

Firm Administration and Staff

The average person on the street may assume lawyers, as well educated legal scholars, are inherently blessed with superior business administration skills. The average lawyer may assume this as well. Like everything in business, results vary. Some lawyers are brilliant businesspeople and others could not successfully consult for their kid's lemonade stand. Quite a few lawyers have absolutely no work experience in the business world prior to becoming a lawyer and no formal education on business issues. For some new lawyers the most complicated budgeting they've been engaged in might have been during their first years in college, saving enough of their monthly allowance to have a better time during Spring Break. Indeed, some lawyers have never even held a real job outside of their clerkship until they start their first position as an Associate. It's no surprise that some encounter difficulties when they find themselves suddenly thrust into supervisory issues or complicated business decisions which can impact the firm's financial performance.

There's nothing shameful in this, it simply shows the reality that business training is not a prerequisite for working at or even owning a law practice. We've already established that good attorneys don't want to spend too much time focused on all the minutia of business operations. It's why they hire staff and legal administrators. Even many senior attorneys with decades of business experience leave administration to the non-lawyers because it allows them to focus on their higher purpose as a lawyer. The simple goal of legal administration goes beyond just running the operations — it's keeping attorneys focused on their critical tasks and the development of their practice. It's the classic opportunity cost decision. Staff can almost always do the non-legal work more efficiently which allows the attorney more time to bill.

Do you know all the details of the licensing of the 50+ applications and specialty software required by various practices at your firm? Do you know the terms of the dozen different insurance policies that your firm has? How about the interest rate on your firm's line of credit? Do you know how many vendors your firm has in place, or how many days of advance notice is required to avoid automatic renewals? Or how many different items appear on your general ledger, and how they are budgeted, measured and evaluated? Do you want or need to know all these details? Probably not. It is why firms hire administrators, so they can handle these issues, so you can focus on practicing law. Staff can be a huge support to your daily life. If you treat them poorly they can also throw a major wrench into your plans.

For many years at mid-size or larger law firms the ratio of attorneys to staff was approximately one to one. For every attorney billing time there was a correlating staffer handling all the aspects of daily business operations. In the past many of the tasks were more labor intensive. You needed a small army of staffers to run a decent sized law firm. As technology advanced the headcount in some departments was reduced. Some staff positions have gone away completely, disappearing with the carbon paper, typewriters, and banks of fax machines. Outsourcing lower paid staff positions has become common. Technology continues to change how the business works and the number of staff positions per lawyer has been slowly decreasing.

If you can, find a copy of the firm's org chart to give yourself an idea of who does what. By understanding who has access and information, you'll be a better judge of the things you hear and see. If you pay attention you'll get the big picture of who has authority, who has information, and who might be able to offer you helpful insight and tips to enhance your career. Law firms have all the administrative departments you would find in any other professional service firm. There are secretaries, accounting personnel, people in marketing, Human Resources, an IT department, and so on. There are also other positions specific to the law practice, such as case clerks, litigation support personnel, and paralegals. Although the staff typically make considerably less than their attorney counterparts they are no less important. Law firms are too cheap to hire extraneous positions. If you encounter under-utilized staff it is usually because the position is poorly managed.

Your first contact with admin will likely be with the HR department since they are charged with talent acquisition, interviewing, managing clerkships, etc. Your connection with them will last well beyond your orientation. Part of their job is to help retain good talent, so they have a professional interest in your success. They are also required to protect the firm's best interests, so if there is anything inappropriate going on at the firm they will play a role in the investigation. You can trust them, but you should know that they have to respond if they see an actionable issue. HR personnel can't (or shouldn't) turn a blind eye to serious policy violations or illegal action. If you share such a concern with your friend in the HR department don't expect your friendship to get in the way of their duty.

There will be staff in various departments which will help you from time to time, but many may not have the bandwidth to help you much. Marketing personnel will be there to get you started on your way with a great headshot and a profile on your firm's webpage. Beyond that don't expect a lot of one-on-one work to help you build your personal brand and a client base unless your firm invests a lot in marketing staff. Most of their efforts will be at a higher level supporting the firm as a whole, or Partners with important clients. If they offer training classes, be sure to take them because they do have valuable information.

One of the best staff connections you will have early on is your secretary, if you are assigned one. Secretarial staffing models have changed over the years. Up until the 1980s it was not uncommon for a Partner to be assigned a personal secretary. Some really important Partners had two secretaries. The one-to-one ratio was nothing shocking back then, but it is rarely seen anymore. These days a legal secretary supporting 4 or 5 attorneys is commonplace. Some support 9 or 10. Some firms have returned to the old typing pool model. In those situations, staff resources are pooled and available to whoever needs them. Technology is a huge driver of this change.

It is worth explaining the transformation because many senior attorneys are hard wired to the past. They plateaued at a certain moment on the technology curve and based on their stature with their firms, they received no penalty for entering permanent technological stasis. Because some in the higher ranks are still in power, it's prudent to understand the world from their point of view to better understand how they work in the modern era. You might be surprised by what you find at your firm. Will you see secretaries printing out emails for their senior Partners to read? Possibly. Will the Partner expect to have unfettered access to their secretary whenever they want? Most likely. Old school secretaries are still highly valued by old school Partners.

Technology has changed the secretary role more than any other, but they are still important. As a new Associate it's wise to avoid the temptation of assuming that your assigned secretary is *your* own personal secretary. Secretaries are paired with several lawyers and the most senior ones receive the majority of their attention. If your assigned secretary is also working for a very senior Partner, you should lower your expectations of support. You may not get any. It's not that the secretary is unwilling to help you, it's often that they cannot do much because of the workload and constant attention required by the Partner.

In the pre-computer world secretaries took dictation, often in shorthand and used those notes to type a letter. Of course, in the days before email all correspondence was handled this way. You can imagine how busy secretaries were. Eventually, tape-recording technology allowed for taped instruction any hour of the day. Lawyers could dictate notes after hours and leave a stack of the tapes for their secretaries to transcribe. Secretaries found themselves wearing headphones half the day, advancing and rewinding cassette tapes with a corded pedal at their feet. It seems almost primitive by today's standards.

Despite the changing role, legal secretaries are still important. Disrespecting a secretary is a rookie mistake. It's not just poor manners, it's poor business. As a new attorney, it's important to realize that creating friction with a valued secretary is a losing position. Put another way, from the perspective of a senior attorney, a great secretary is hard to find. Associates are minted daily. New Associates should not over-estimate their own importance when finding themselves in a conflict situation with a secretary. Some Partners have strong feelings about who is more valuable to the organization.

A secretary with decades of experience knows a great deal about the practical application of law. With different inclinations or resources earlier in life, they might have gone to law school themselves. Secretaries will provide assistance even if they are busy because many will work above and beyond the call of duty. Loyal secretaries who feel appreciated will volunteer to come in early or work late when you need their help. If you treat them like part of the team and truly create a respectful and mutually symbiotic relationship, you'll start your legal career with much needed allies. It's not hard to find attorneys who have been with the same secretaries for decades.

Paralegals remain vital to many practices. They have important roles supporting both transactional and controversy practices. Some high volume, form-based practices like corporate immigration would not be profitable without them. The technology changes in law have affected paralegal positions as well. In the past litigation was excessively manually intensive. A huge discovery production might produce hundreds of boxes of documents. Paralegals would spread out in war rooms and touch each document to physically inspect it. Using a device similar to an old pricing gun from a grocery store, they would manually stamp pages with a Bates labeler, giving each document its own unique number as a possible exhibit in the case. The documents were copied, indexed and manually searched for anything that held the glimmer of relevance. Fast forward and those who now bate stamp do so electronically. In fact, most of those new to the paralegal profession may not have ever seen a manual Bates stamper first hand.

The top administrative director at your firm may have the title of Chief Operations Officer (COO), Executive Director, or Firm Administrator. Often these individuals have an MBA, CPA, or HR certification. The position effectively manages overall operations at the direction of the firm's Executive or Management Committee. At some firms these individuals have considerable authority and incredible access to information. At other firms they are essentially office managers. It depends on the goals and structure of the firm. Legal administrators, directors and managers oversee departmental functions and act as the stewards of your firm's resources. They play a big role in how firm expenses are managed and how money is spent.

Law firms tend to hire managers and directors who come from within the legal industry. Although most firms claim they will consider employees from outside of legal, they typically favor candidates from within the industry, believing that they have some special insight to the needs of attorneys. There are many excellent managers, but like many industries, legal has its share of average managers who will follow your every command, even when you give poor direction. They aren't going to risk their jobs fighting for most issues. Exceptional managers will push back, respectfully, when you give them instructions that are contrary to their better business judgement. For example, good IT managers will push back if told to not spend any money on IT projects in the coming year. They know the inherent long-term risks associated with under-investment. One law firm had to deal with a very public dispute with a former client because it was using outdated remote access software. The software in question was no longer supported and exploits, which could allow unauthorized network access, had been published on the internet. The inaction that allowed the issue to occur in the first place was cause enough for alarm. That firm may have had inadequate IT support, or they may have had frustrated technology managers who were unable to secure the necessary funding to do things right. Regardless of the circumstances, that firm had to defend itself in a lawsuit. The story hit the national media and created a huge distraction for everyone at the firm.

Keeping staff well-paid and well-trained isn't cheap but it's one of the best investments to make. A strong staff can help make firms more efficient and prosperous. Firms which take this for granted do so at their own risk. Some firms don't pay attention to the needs of their staff and they struggle with high turnover. The churn of employees not only hurts morale, it can put a practice at risk if it ends up with poorly trained employees. A courier could fail to deliver an important document timely. A secretary could send an overnight package to the wrong party. An e-discovery specialist could miss a major parameter of a search required for production. Even a receptionist could offend a client or opposing counsel. Every position is important, and many of them could produce disaster or even unwittingly allow a firm to commit malpractice if they fail in their duties. It is for that reason firms need competent legal managers to ensure that everyone is doing their job. Good departmental and line management help ensure the business runs smoothly.

There are some simple ways to create a strong relationship with the staff. Start with basic appreciation. Take time to get to know them. Knowing when your secretary's birthday lands is a good thing. Learning the birthday dates of their spouse or children is even better. Shifting your own schedule a bit to allow a secretary time to get to a school event or an anniversary dinner shows a sensitivity that is sure to be appreciated. While most lawyers will take care of their own direct reports don't forget about the other departments. Doing something nice for the accounting department, office services, or the library department will go a long way as well. Cards, thank you notes, flowers on birthdays, and gifts during administrative professional week are all thoughtful efforts which can help create a lasting relationship. A random box of donuts can show you appreciate their service. Lawyers shouldn't hesitate to dip into their own pockets to share the wealth with their assistants during the holidays. While most law firms have some type of year-end bonus system in place, a small but thoughtful token of appreciation goes a long way.

19

The Seven Year Trap

If you strive to be an owner of a law firm someday, you will encounter obstacles and pitfalls on your way to equity partnership. Many of the scenarios you will meet are not designed to be malevolent, they are simply situations which can occur to the uninformed. You can avoid career delays and distractions by looking out for the signs which may indicate trouble is ahead. Most importantly, you need to know what the firm really requires for promotion.

"The Seven Year Trap" is a scenario which plays out far too frequently during the normal career progression of Associates as they work toward their ultimate goal of becoming an Equity Partner. It is a series of events and decisions which Associate lawyers confront whether they realize it or not. The trap isn't something that you suddenly step on, like a landmine that explodes if you take a wrong step. The trap is a meandering pathway. It's littered with financial rewards which make you think you're heading in the right direction. You'll keep moving in that direction for seven years, the traditional duration for an Associate position. If you fall into the trap at the end of the line you either won't be promoted, or you will get a promotion that essentially flatlines your career.

How can a promotion be a career flatline? Let's start at the beginning. Most people understand there is a timeline for career progression from "baby lawyer" to seasoned Partner. The general assumption is that hard work is the primary requirement and after many years of it you'll be rewarded with a promotion. From the first day of employment, much of your time will be directed by others. Even so, new lawyers will still have to make their own decisions which will have a cumulative impact on the direction of their career. Often the decisions have consequences which may not be apparent for months or years to come. Complicating things is a reward structure for young attorneys which can send mixed signals, encouraging certain behaviors and actions. Some of the behavior that is strongly encouraged at the start of your career can be detrimental in the later phases. This is precisely why you need to enter the profession forewarned.

Traditionally, Associates follow a common route through college, law school, and the commencement of their first job. At the start of their career their primary focus will be on day-to-day issues. Their world will be entirely centered on finding work and completing assignments. Partnership is a long way off and understandably the criteria for promotion is not on the top of their mind when they're just getting started. They're focused on survival, and they aren't alone. At this point most first-year lawyers are simply content with having a good job.

As they near their emotionally significant thirties, many Associates are living a life just like everyone else in the business world. They're possibly in a serious personal relationship. They're starting to see the world now that they make enough money to take the occasional vacation. They are thinking about the financial considerations of buying their first home. Maybe they have a nice new car. At this point some may start thinking about having kids. Typical Associates who survive the first few years employed at good law firms can become very comfortable with the world they live in. Work seems pretty good and up to this point the career has been rewarding. With each raise they often adjust their lifestyle. Why work so hard if you can't enjoy the rewards, right? The workloads might be tough from time to time, but most things seem comfortable and predictable, for now.

Year 6 comes along and Associates on the traditional path begin to hear the question more often: Are you on the partnership track? They assume they are. They've never missed their billable hour goal. Week after week, month after month they worked hard and met the requirements for their job. They learned some rules early: Hit your hours budget to keep your job, surpass it if you want a big bonus. And they worked hard! When other people left early for happy hour, they stayed in their office to grind out work. While other people were sending photos from their extended vacation in Asia, the hard-working Associate was toiling through another lunch at their desk. Over the years they got good evaluations and they were continually rewarded with raises and bonuses. They had no big problems and their mentors never mentioned any concerns. After seven years of dedicated effort their firm announces the list of those up for promotion and surprise, they are not on the list. What happened?

It seems counter-intuitive, but if you fit the description above, your faith and work-ethic might have inadvertently hampered your partnership prospects. In exceptionally busy law firms your willingness to work hard will likely get you noticed and that may produce a steady flow of work opportunities. That sounds good though, doesn't it? Not necessarily. It can be a pie eating contest where the winner gets more pie.

If you are a litigation Associate and enjoy doing document review, you may get more document review opportunities than you can handle. If you are good at the tasks and receptive to the work, your firm may allow you to do document review year-in, year-out, for years. No one will stop you from doing this. It sure feels like a path to success. The more hours you work, the bigger bonuses you may get. But that isn't a long-term strategy for career development. Solely focusing on the work, especially lower level legal work, is the source of the problem for many. Few people become an Equity Partner on the strength of their hard work alone. For most firms it is rare to get promoted to the ownership ranks unless you have your own clients and a sustainable book of business.

Most firms have a two-tier partnership structure; Non-Equity Partner and Equity Partner. It is possible to be promoted to non-equity status by simply paying your dues and working really hard for seven or eight years. Many lawyers reach this first level of partnership and stay there for the rest of their careers. If you don't develop clients your career will likely remain at this plateau.

It's important to have legitimate expectations because the requirements and rewards vary from firm to firm. Being promoted to Non-Equity Partner at your firm may be a big deal, or it may simply be a social promotion that everyone receives after a certain amount of years in practice. Most firms will not require a personal capital contribution to become a Non-Equity. The cost of promoting you to the non-equity level is fairly low. In addition to a better title, your pay usually increases, and you might even receive better benefits. The firm is okay with this because they will bill you out at a higher rate now that you are a Partner. That is a double edged blade. Your increased billing rates might help you produce more revenue, but it may also reduce the amount of work you are assigned because some Equity Partners may stop using you if your rates become too high for their clients. Or they may bill you out with steep discounts.

As a Non-Equity Partner your compensation is likely to correlate directly with your productivity and collections. Hard work should be enough to grant you some security, but there are few long term guarantees. If your only contribution to the firm is the hours you work, you may be at risk if your hours decline. If you are promoted solely by virtue of cranking out billable hours, you may be forced to sustain that level of effort for the rest of your career just to maintain your position or compensation level. Your base pay will likely cap out at some point. Once that occurs the only compensation variable will be your bonus, and you'll have to work hard to get it. You shouldn't expect those annual raises like you received as an Associate. The firm will have some constraints. For example, they are unlikely to pay you a base salary much higher than the rates set for the junior Equity Partners.

Being a Non-Equity Partner is great, until it isn't. If times get tough and the firm has layoffs, you might be at greater risk because you are more expensive than all the Associates. You may be viewed as a threat to the Associates in your section because you are sucking up all the good projects which should be going to someone at their level. As an employee outside of the ownership group you have no protection if times get tough. If an Equity Partner who supported you over the years leaves your firm, you may be left exposed and unprotected.

The traps in this business don't just snare young lawyers, they trip up seasoned lawyers as well. If you are completely reliant on others to feed you work as a Non-Equity Partner, you may find yourself out of a job in your late 50s or early 60s. There are lawyers who find themselves without a position late in life, just a few years before they planned to retire. It's brutal to be cast out after a lifetime of sacrifice and hard work. The sad reality is the work you do as a 30-year attorney can probably be done by a 10-year attorney, for a much cheaper price. High paid service lawyers are often easy targets for firms who need to cut costs.

If you want long term job security, you have to be an owner. To become one, you have to take a different path. You can't avoid the basic requirements early in your career, but at some point, you must pivot your focus towards client development. You have to accept the reality of the shrinking sands in the hourglass. You have 7 years to get promoted, maybe 8 if you are lucky. It's not an arbitrary number of years. The position of Associate isn't meant to be a lifelong position for most people. Take a moment and look at a few websites of the big law firms you know. Check the year of law school graduation dates of all the Associate profiles they list. You should notice that there are very few Associates who graduated law school more than 10 years before. By year 7 or 8 most private practice firms decide on whether you are going to advance to the next level. By that point in their careers some lawyers find themselves in an "up or out" scenario, meaning they either move up to a higher-level position or they move out of the firm. Even if you aren't progressing, after seven years some firms will promote you to Non-Equity Partner, or they may call you Of Counsel or Senior Attorney. That can feel like a comfortable plateau, but it can be a career flatline. That's the trap.

Why does the trap even exist? Law firms need you to keep producing as much as possible and they will pay you to do so, for as long as it continues to make financial sense. The trap exists because law firms won't encourage you to do the required client development work necessary over the years because they need

160

you to focus on billing hours. They can't wait for you to be profitable in 7 years. They need you to make them money now. Most of the early rewards you will receive are for your short-term success producing hours and are not indicators that you are ready to become a Partner. Those rewards were really just proof that you've been a productive Associate.

Law firms are under major pressure to be profitable. The world of law firm finance follows a 12-month calendar. Annual profitability is what helps the firm attract and retain the best people. In a hyper-competitive environment, one bad year of reduced profits may be just bad enough to discourage good laterals from joining. It may be bad enough to pull a thread from the fabric that is holding a law firm together. That may sound like an exaggeration, but many successful law firms have fallen apart with dizzying speed. While powerful law firms are strong enough to focus simultaneously on short-term profitability and long-term sustainability, most others are not. They are driven by annual profits and this reality has helped set the 7 year trap.

Many law firms won't stop you from focusing too much energy on low level work. If you are willing to be pigeon-holed, you can get stuck on a treadmill. You'll be moving, but not moving forward. Don't confuse activity with productivity. Be careful not to trade vital steps in your career path for the short term bonus gains for cranking out work. You need to find a variety of projects that challenge you. If you don't ask for better assignments over the years, you may end up on the path of least resistance doing second year level work for the next 7 years. To avoid the trap, you need to hit year seven with a strong skill set and some serious time invested in client development.

As an Associate, things are only good as long as you make the firm money, or as long as they see your potential to make them money. Everything is masked by culture. You may love your firm. You may feel that your firm loves you back, but it can't. The firm is a thing, it has no emotion. Although the people around you may care for you dearly, in the end the firm has to make decisions based on an economic justification. With each passing year your contribution margins are watched closer. Each year that you work for a firm you become more expensive. Every year your cost to the firm goes up with raises and increased benefit costs. The firm's rent goes up, as well as most everything else they pay for. Ideally, each year your standard rates increase a bit to offset the costs. But the industry is more competitive now and some clients are very price sensitive. Private practice law firms live and die by the margins. No firm has the luxury of ignoring the numbers. Like it or not, you are a number.

How do you avoid the trap? How do you build clients in an environment that doesn't encourage or support your efforts? You start by proving yourself. For the first two to three years focus mostly on hard work. View everything as a learning opportunity. Earn a reputation and the respect of your peers and your boss by being a producer. Keep your head down and work. Take some client development action, but don't embark on any major plan that will take you away from the very critical working and learning phase of your career. Not everyone survives this phase, so it's important to focus on hours and the development of your skills. Your hard work is an investment. If you aren't exhausted from time to time, you are doing something wrong.

After you have billed about 5,000 hours of good work you will hit a stage of credibility in the eyes of your employer. At this time try to redirect some of your free capacity into client development. If you don't have any free time, consider regulating your workload to allow for more time dedicated to client development efforts, while never falling below the expected minimum billable expectation. You want to start on business development sooner than later because the big results can take years to achieve. By shifting some of your focus to building a client base, you may be billing less than your colleagues, but that is okay as long as you are billing more than the stated minimum requirement.

At this stage your efforts to land clients are more about creating contacts. You are simply dipping your toes in the waters of business development. By the time you get out of law school your peers who started work after getting a business undergraduate degree are already three years into their careers. By the time you are a mid-level Associate the same peers are entering management and becoming decision makers in their own companies. Even if they aren't the direct purchasers of legal services they often know someone who is. Business people want to work with people they trust. The relationships you nurture early on in your professional life can be valuable for your entire career. Don't worry about the limited results early on. No one is expecting you to land a great client at this stage anyway. You are just planting seeds. In fact, many of the client opportunities you do encounter early on may not be at the level your firm is willing to engage, especially if you are at a large firm.

Turning your attention away from your hours, even if it's just a small portion might seem wrong, especially if your peers are hitting big hours. If you are beating your billable requirement, you'll be okay. Law firms rarely fire Associates who consistently beat their hours, especially if your total commitment (billable and non-billable work) shows how dedicated you are.

If your firm requires 1,800 billable hours a year you should invest at least 2,450 hours a year in total. 2,450 total hours sounds like a lot. It's about 50 hours a week. That means you won't be working 9 to 5. Most Partners didn't work 9 to 5 when they started either. You may occasionally have to work late or put in some weekend time. If you take a vacation, you'll have to make that time up. Don't underestimate the cumulative value of your experience. Under the example below, by the time you are up for Partner you have 13,550 hours of billable experience — more than enough to work at a Partner level. You also have 1,500 hours invested into your own business development plan.

	Billable Hours	NB Hours	BD Hours	Total Hours
Year 1	2,050	300	100	2,450
Year 2	2,050	300	100	2,450
Year 3	1,950	300	200	2,450
Year 4	1,900	300	250	2,450
Year 5	1,900	300	250	2,450
Year 6	1,850	300	300	2,450
Year 7	1,850	300	300	2,450

What if you can't find enough work to hit those billable hours? If you can't hit your minimum work requirement contact your supervisor, mentor, section head, or Managing Partner. If you can't find work in your section, volunteer for projects in other sections or even other offices. If you still can't find enough billable work, invest all your unallocated billing time into business development and training efforts.

Many of your fellow Associates are going to be so obsessed with hours that they won't begin their own business development efforts until it is too late. At the end of the day your extra time on a random file won't be worth the time you have invested in marketing your services and obtaining your own clients. Those early bonuses for crazy high hours won't seem so great later to your peers who flatline as a Non-Equity. They may spend the next 30 years of their career wishing they had clients, but they may be too busy trying to do the work of others just to stay afloat.

If you realize the need to secure clients late on your path, don't sacrifice all your productivity to make up for missed client development time. I've seen many a 6-year lawyer launch into a full-scale business development plan to rectify the impact of years of inaction. They often over-correct and spend so much time on marketing outreach that they miss their minimum hours requirement. They can fall deeper into the trap. At this point if you don't have clients the one facet of your practice that is valued by the firm is your productivity and if that suffers you may be at greater risk. If you feel the need to invest 600 hours a year into creating your own practice, make sure that effort occurs in addition to meeting your minimum billable hour requirement.

The 7 year trap gives you a false sense of security that your hard work is enough to be a Partner. It's not enough to make you an Equity Partner. It's also not enough to protect you for your entire career. Avoid the trap by starting early on your plan to obtain clients. In the end having clients and a healthy book of business will protect you and create opportunities. You can have control over your destiny if you have control over your own business. The sooner you start working on that, the better.

20
Other Traps on Your Path

In addition to "The Seven Year Trap," you'll encounter other situations which can impact your career or promotion prospects, including notable scenarios such as:

- The Take Over My Practice once I Retire Trap
- The Don't Bill those Hours Trap
- The Non-Billable Work Trap
- The I Value Loyalty Trap
- The My Partner Protects Me Trap
- The Come with Me to Another Firm Trap
- The Billing Partner Trap
- The Non-Replication Trap

These traps may not kill your career, but they certainly can slow you down or create additional stress in your life.

The Take Over My Practice once I Retire Trap occurs when a senior Partner convinces you to hitch your wagon to their practice. Instead of developing your own book of business you'll need to dedicate all your time and efforts in supporting their clients. They promise to hand over their book of business to you at some point in the future. It sounds reasonable because it is entirely plausible, and for some folks the promises are actually fulfilled. For others though the promises are not kept, or at the very least the timeline was significantly longer than what was promised. I have challenged 100% of the attorneys I know who claim they will retire in 2 or 3 years. That's because most don't. I know a lot of people who told me they would retire in a couple of years 10 years ago and they are still working. The truth is some Partners won't retire until they absolutely have to do so. Many successful Partners have sweet deals near the end of their career, allowing them to wind down at leisure while still getting paid. Why would anyone in such a situation walk away if they are well compensated and not expected to work as much?

If you are in this situation take a deeper look at the Partner's actions. Are there any realistic signs that they are actually going to slow down and transition their clients to you? If so, you should be taking greater responsibility with the client. Are you getting more direct calls and covering for your Partner more often as they reduce their workloads? These are good signs. Your goal in this situation is to have the client think of you first when they call your firm. Partners who are truly interested in transitioning their practice take a clear stance and ensure that the client is comfortable with the eventual handoff. Partners may continue to manage the relationship at a high level, but you'll be doing all the work. Everyone on the client team should know that you'll be taking over if the handover plan is genuine.

If on the other hand, you see no changes and your Partner continues to work hard and control every aspect of the client relationship, you may simply remain a service lawyer. If your access or knowledge of the client doesn't change much over time be careful putting all your eggs in that basket — you may be sacrificing your own client development opportunities to support someone else's practice. Even if your Partner has good intentions, they don't always control the ultimate destiny of a client. Is the Partner slowing down, or is their entire practice simply grinding to a halt? It's entirely possible that the client's work has run its course and will end when the Partner retires. If new leadership takes control of the client's operations, the new management of that company may simply change law firms to their own existing contacts. As you develop a closer relationship with the Partner you will learn more and more details on the client and the long-term plan. Don't be afraid to ask about their expectations. If they are sincere in their promises to you, they shouldn't be concerned about discussing the future.

The Don't Bill Those Hours Trap happens when a Partner tells you not to bill time for a matter they aren't offering helpful advice, they are most likely skirting around their own firm's accounting rules. They do it to make their own clients happy and to make their own numbers seem more profitable. It's one thing to write off time as a discount to a client. That happens quite often. It's completely another thing for a Partner to prohibit the recording of time worked. That is rarely appropriate and unfortunately it is not uncommon. All time should be recorded whether it will ultimately be billed or not. It's the only way for a firm to be able to determine what the costs of services sold are. Without complete and honest data, an unprofitable client can seem profitable. The bad thing about this situation is that very few people in administration or your section will have your back if you push the issue. Don't question it and you may get stuck doing a lot of work for free going forward. Push too hard and you risk upsetting the Partner.

Each situation is different but don't fall into the trap of being a Partner's permanent subsidy for their client. If a Partner tells you not to record time on a matter once, odds are they will do it again later. You are effectively operating as an off-the-books discount for their client. All their time will be recorded. They know that your future success at the firm is going to be based on your numbers, and some of them just don't care. Preserving their client's favor, and protecting their own numbers, is more important to them than the potentially negative impact an Associate may encounter. It's rare, but some Partners may view you as a disposable commodity.

If a Partner is doing this and is challenged by administration they may claim writing off your time was necessary because you billed more than what was acceptable, or they'll insist the quality of the work wasn't good enough. Few people will challenge a Partner's assessment of the quality of your work.

As a young lawyer it is very difficult to tell a Partner that you won't work on their projects. The last thing you want is for a Partner to be annoyed with you. If the Partner insists that you not record billable time, try to record it as non-billable. That way when your numbers are reviewed it will be apparent that you are working, even though you aren't generating revenue. At this stage of your career no one expects you to bring in major collections, but the further you go, the higher the expectations rise. Firms will look at your total effort so non-billable time matters too. Fail to record that time and it may appear you aren't working hard enough.

The Non-Billable Work Trap sneaks up on you. You already know that non-billable work is an unavoidable component of your practice. Some Partners will view this as a source for free work, similar to the don't bill your hours scenario. In this case you are permitted to record the time you work, but it will be allocated to something like business development or marketing. People will ask you to look quickly at a matter for them, but they have no intention of billing the time for your effort. If this happens frequently your personal metrics may suffer.

Also, be mindful of your legitimate administrative commitments, especially if you are having trouble hitting your billable requirement. It is unlikely that anyone will stop you from taking on too many non-billable commitments at first. Agreeing to participate in something like the summer clerkship programs or on campus recruiting can take you away from your desk quite a bit. It's important to be engaged but do not overextend yourself if your workload is shaky or if you have a major project coming up. If you have a major trial about to commence the last thing you want to do is to spread yourself too thin with non-billable responsibilities. Be sure to ask for billable numbers whenever anyone asks you to do work. If you are short on billable hours, tell them so. At the end of the year if you miss your hours by a wide margin no one will come to your defense and say, "but look at those great non-billables."

The I Value Loyalty Trap may not seem like a trap initially. Loyalty is valued everywhere. The people you work with need to know that you will honor your commitments, and even make sacrifices when necessary. However, sometimes when someone tells you they value loyalty it isn't as honorable as they make it seem. What it really means is they value your loyalty to them personally, not to the firm or anyone else. What they want is your undivided attention, your unwavering support, and your unconditional willingness to do whatever they tell you to do. That loyalty may not be reciprocal. Be careful with Partners who regularly beat this drum. You don't want to set yourself up to be someone's fall guy. I've known Partners who appear to have never made an error in their professional life because every single mistake, even the small ones, were pinned on their Associates.

You will encounter Partners who are only in this business for themselves, and they may test your loyalty. Tread carefully because the leadership of your firm is probably watching a Partner like this more than other Partners. It's very easy to become labeled as part of a specific team or camp. If your Partner is suspected as being on the fence, or outright disloyal to the firm, you may be viewed in a similar manner if all your work comes from that Partner.

Your best course of action is to be mindful of what is being asked of you. If you have an uneasy feeling about your Partner's motives, try to get assignments from other Partners if you can. You may not have many opportunities to distance yourself, especially if you need the work. Discreetly changing your focus to others can create risks for you, but it's better to risk losing favor with a particular Partner early on, rather than later. In the unlikely event that your Partner is doing something inappropriate, you may find solace with your section head or other firm leaders.

The My Partner Protects Me Trap catches Associates who get too comfortable with a Partner. A strong Partner can be a great mentor and advocate for you at your firm. Once you earn the trust and respect of a Partner they may be a dependable source of work for you. You may land in an enviable position, at least from the perspective of other Associates. Being well-regarded by a Partner who views you as their personal Associate can create opportunities for you. You can get great work assignments and have greater access to information. You'll have someone who will go to bat for you if issues ever rise up. You may think of the Partner as "my Partner." In reality, you are "their Associate."

While it can be great to be part of a team led by a successful Partner there can be a downside, so don't get too comfortable. Don't take advantage of this situation and assume that you don't have to worry about the typical responsibilities of your position. Senior Partners can become territorial when it comes to ensuring the availability of their team. You may become branded as untouchable to other Partners. This can narrow your focus into a single practice area. If 100% of your work comes from a Partner by default your practice will develop in their niche. That's not a bad thing, especially if you are prepared to leverage that experience to develop a focus in that area. Hopefully, you enjoy the work because you may become typecast.

While it is great to develop a specialty under the guidance of a strong Partner, working for many Partners early on will expose you to a broader range of practices and issues. It's always good early in your career to meet as many people as possible to build a broad reputation as a solid member of the firm. When you are up for promotion all of your firm's Equity Partners are likely to vote on whether or not you get promoted. If the majority of your work has been done for a single person, much of your case for promotion rests in their hands. It's helpful to have more than one Equity Partner capable of speaking your praises.

Lastly, there are a few Associates who get cocky and disregard a firm's mores and norms if they feel protected by their boss. If you treat people poorly or disregard them because you feel protected by an important Partner, you may be inviting trouble. I have worked with Associates who were completely disrespectful to others at the firm because they were certain they were untouchable due to their close relationship with a big Partner. These Associates claimed they worked for the Partner, not the firm. In many cases when the Partner finally departed they left alone, abandoning the Associate to a very short and unpleasant experience in their final days at the firm. It's a good reminder that your reputation will follow you throughout your entire career. Many of your fellow Associates will be Partners in the future here and at other firms across town and across the nation. It's amazing how many people will remember your actions so always try to be considerate and professional.

The Come with Me to Another Firm Trap happens more to Associates who have a strong bond to a Partner. Partners do occasionally resign, move to other firms, and take their teams with them. If a Partner at your firm is unhappy and looking for other opportunities, you may hear scuttlebutt about their dissatisfaction and search for a new home. Don't feel betrayed if a Partner you work closely with didn't mention their exit plans to you earlier. They have a fiduciary responsibility as an owner of their current firm, so they really shouldn't be recruiting for their future firm until the existing bond is officially broken.

Partners lateral to other firms all the time. Most Partners at your firm are targeted continually, especially those with a large book of business. Good lawyers are continuously approached by recruiters offering a better deal. Partners who do leave have a lot of leverage when they join another firm and they can often bring Associates and staff with them. You may or may not be asked to join a departing Partner. It all depends on your role on the team and the appetite of the firm. If the destination firm is well stocked with Associates the lateral Partner may not be able to bring with them all or any of their chosen Associates.

This can be a difficult scenario no matter what happens. If you get the majority of your work from a single Partner and they leave your firm, you may end up in an awkward situation when they ask you to leave with them. The Partner who is leaving may give you very little notice of the pending change, so you may have to make a snap decision, giving you precious little time to weigh your options. That can be a problem because your current firm may react in quick order.

If Partners in your practice area depart, your firm should make an immediate assessment of the impact. Your firm should approach you as soon as the move is announced, but they may need time to examine the impact more. Not all firm management is adept at dealing with personnel defections. Whenever a very important Partner leaves emotions can flare. If your section remains viable after the departure of the Partner, your firm may reach out and confirm their desire to keep you. Or they may question your loyalty, assuming that you knew about your Partner's resignation ahead of time. If your entire section leaves and you remain behind your firm will have to figure out what to do with you. If they see a reason for you to stay, they will lobby to keep you. Your firm may try to reassign you, or they may simply terminate you if you are no longer needed.

If you find yourself in the middle of two firms who want you, there's a huge decision to make. If there is still work for you to do at your current firm this will be an opportunity to prove your loyalty if you don't leave. Your existing firm can claim a victory by limiting the number of people who left with the departing Partner. It is possible but unlikely that you'll be able to get a raise or promotion as a condition of staying, but you will win favor. Demanding anything from your current firm during this difficult situation may appear like a bit of a shakedown. At this time firm leadership is watching for signs of your loyalty to the firm. If you try to sweeten your deal you may come across as mercenary. They won't forget how you react during this tough moment.

If the departing Partner wants you to come with them, try to get the best offer possible. Making a lateral move may be the best deal you can get, but often these moves present an opportunity to increase your pay, or to even get promoted into a Non-Equity Partner role if you are close to being promoted at your current firm. Be careful not to put yourself into another box. Try to get insight into why the Partner left in the first place. Is the new firm building something big that you can be a part of? Or did your old firm fire your Partner for some very troubling reason? Ask a lot of questions and keep your eyes wide open. These opportunities are usually very short lived, so you won't have much time to ponder the outcomes. The transition can be cordial, or it can be dramatic and emotional. Some Partners who resign are ordered to vacate the premises immediately. It can be an awkward situation.

The Billing Partner Trap can happen if you simply sit back and rely on your faith in the system. Some firms do not allow Associates to be in charge of a client matter. In those firms every client or client matter must be assigned a billing Partner. Be careful with this one if you develop a client as an Associate. It's not unusual for firms to want to have a Partner oversee all matters. Often a Partner will simply have and administrative role to monitor your bills, and perhaps even your work. That's not a problem. The problem occurs if the client grows and the firm forgets who brought in the client in the first place. In many firms there is credit given based on who owns the book, yet some accounting systems are not sophisticated enough to list both an originating Associate and an administrative billing Partner. During your reviews make sure your supervisors know about any client you brought in. Don't let your success silently go to the credit of a Partner. Be sure to track every dollar you bring in — and not just the value of your own work. You want to track the total value of all the timekeepers on your client. This will help tell the story of why you should be an Equity Partner.

The Replication Trap can happen to you if you work in a smaller firm. Despite their best intentions, some firms have a set lifespan. In smaller operations with strong founders, that life span is usually 25 to 35 years. New law firms are often created by a limited group of younger Partners who set out on their own after developing their careers at another firm. They start their firm with a decent foundation and an established client base. The shared experiences of starting a new venture can create tight bonds that last their entire career. Unfortunately, even firms with a great start aren't guaranteed to last forever, so if you join them as an Associate the firm may not be around for your entire career. Many firms last only one generation and die once the founders resign or slow down.

These firms fail to replicate a second generation of leadership and rainmakers. The common aspect of firms in this trap is a centralized control of power and an overreliance on the status quo. Some of the firms in this trap are averse to growth opportunities but others may add quite a few lawyers to help manage the work. In either scenario the power of the original founders does not really change. The founders of these firms control everything, and they are very comfortable with the status quo. They don't have any interest in expanding the ownership ranks much because they don't want to split firm profits further. Unfortunately, for the younger lawyers at these firms, there may not be much investment in the development of the skills and opportunities necessary to run the firms themselves someday. The founding Partners protect their clients and their own income by holding everything close to the vest.

While there is nothing wrong with being a service lawyer, if you aren't an owner in a firm like this it's really important to have accurate expectations on what the future holds so you can plan for the eventual transition. You can make a fair prediction that most lawyers will retire in their mid-to-late-60s or early 70s. If your Partners appear to be within a few years of retirement there should be a lot of discussion about what happens after they retire. If no one is discussing the future and succession plans, you are in a trap.

If most of the rainmaking and management is handled by a small group at the top, the firm can suffer as that group ages. The sudden departure of a founder can expose a firm that lacks management skills or the ability to generate sufficient new clients. In the end the failure of the original leadership to replicate and nurture a second generation of leaders will ultimately doom the firm. Often younger lawyers assume the founders will simply pass along their business. But there is no guarantee because the client relationship itself changes over time. There are lawyers who dedicate a larger portion of their career to a firm, only to find themselves without a strong foundation once their senior Partners call it a day. Sadly, their confidence in senior leadership can makes some people blind to the long term risks. Often the service lawyers don't realize their predicament until the founders are preparing for retirement.

Throughout your entire career you should keep an eye on the future. Ask yourself where you are going to be in five years. If you don't know the answer, you may need to give your situation a stronger review to ensure your career's long term safety and stability.

21

Someone is Getting Fired. Is it You?

Not all lawyers will find an easy path in this profession. Some will get fired. Being fired from your job can be traumatic for an Associate. Delivering a termination notice is no picnic for the firm either. It's literally the worst part of being an owner or a manager of a firm. No one wants to be involved in a termination meeting. Some of the toughest, harshest lawyers melt like butter when it's time to fire someone. Even the most self-centered, uncaring people are often flushed with empathy when they have to sit face to face with someone to tell them that their employment is being terminated. Firing someone may result in the destruction of their career ambitions. The loss of the job may put them in financial distress and have terrible impacts on their family. Despite the abhorrence to the process, terminations still occur regularly and usually for good reason. When a firm hires a lawyer, they make a financial and emotional investment in that person. If the hiring Partner thought for an instant that you might eventually get fired, they wouldn't have hired you in the first place.

Talent acquisition is time-consuming and expensive, so retention is a big issue for law firms. Think of all of the people involved and the actions which occur in the recruiting process. Résumés and cover letters are reviewed, data is obtained, backgrounds are checked, meetings are coordinated, numerous people take time out of their schedule to attend interview meetings, evaluations are compared, then offers are determined and extended. For each position you can multiply that effort by the number of candidates considered. A Partner who attends several interviews may sacrifice more than half a day's billings.

Once someone is hired an entirely different and expensive process kicks into place. A team of people at the firm will handle the onboarding and training of a new hire. New Associates are given an office or workspace, computers, staff to assist them, and anything else they might need for a successful start at the firm. The commitment is public as well, with press releases and additions to the firm's website. Some sophisticated firms have a year-long program mapped out to ensure the successful transition of new hires. It's a lot of effort to bring new people into the fold. New hires earn compensation from the first moment they arrive, but the firm knows it will be months before they begin to make any money on a new addition. It's an even longer wait until the new hires are actually contributing to the firm's profit. With all the effort invested to acquire the best talent, you can see why law firms don't like letting someone go unless they really have to.

People come, and people go in any business. Firms know some resignations are going to happen. It's an unavoidable reality so firms generally try to create an environment which minimizes departures. They would also prefer not to fire people, so they set up similar mechanisms to help keep their employees in line. Terminations require firms to essentially admit some level of failure. Firing someone can produce extreme emotions at a firm if the action is widely viewed as unjust, which can happen at times because most disciplinary actions leading up to the termination occur in private. Some terminated employees will make accusations of improper firing, discrimination, or retaliation. On rare occasions some employees disagree so strenuously with the termination decision that they will require a security escort out the door. Firms are aware of the threats, so good ones have an entire HR arsenal which they can deploy to correct issues before they take any measure as drastic as a termination.

A minor transgression is generally not enough to get someone fired in most environments. The firm expects you to make some mistakes as you learn the business. They will make course adjustments from time to time, when necessary. Most minor issues are addressed or even overlooked. In fact, depending on the firm, you may have to work really hard to actually get terminated. Every firm is a little different, so you should not be cavalier and make assumptions. At firms with a very strong leader, termination decisions can be instant and implemented swiftly. Other firms with indecisive leadership and weak or ineffective HR can linger on a decision, allowing the poorly performing lawyer to wade deeper into trouble.

As strange as it may sound, you are actually fortunate if you work at a firm that takes disciplinary action when problems arise. In those firms you are lucky because you know what the problems are, and you have an opportunity to address the issues. Other firms are less effective and reactionary. If they think you are going to fail, they may simply try to wait you out. If you aren't causing a disruption, they may hope that poor reviews, skipped raises, or insufficient bonuses will be enough to run you off. It sounds crazy, but some poorly managed firms will stop investing in your future with the hope that you'll get the hint and eventually resign. Don't get comfortable and try to beat them at their own game. Every day that you spend in a firm which has stopped contributing to your growth is a wasted day. As an Associate your career clock is ticking. While you are in limbo your peers are learning valuable skills. If you feel like your career is stagnating or dying on the vine, start to think about other options. Don't be afraid to talk to your supervisors. If you think you are in an unwinnable situation you literally have nothing to lose.

Discipline is not disaster and is often a good thing. If a firm didn't care about you or see your potential, they could simply fire you. Many states are right to work states, which means you can be fired for any reason or no reason, as long as the action wasn't discriminatory. Discipline itself is a surprisingly simple concept. It only feels difficult because of emotions, which is perfectly natural. Every business has performance expectations. If you aren't meeting the expectations, your firm may deploy a set of progressive disciplinary actions designed to fix the problems. You may see the plans play out through coaching, verbal warnings, written warnings, and other actions up to and including termination. Each step of the way the HR people document everything for the file. If the problems are resolved the memos and emails in the file will become benign. If someone is terminated, that file is the firm's best protection if they get sued for wrongful termination.

A quick distinction on the two types of terminations is necessary. There are layoffs and terminations for cause. If times are tough, you may be laid off even though you haven't done anything wrong. Layoffs can occur during economic slowdowns. If you aren't a big producer and your section is slowing down, your firm could terminate you because they don't need you. If you were hired to support a big client and the firm loses that client, you may be a prime candidate for a layoff. Firms don't make such decisions lightly. Often, they have no choice. Layoffs are generally viewed as more compassionate because the firm is essentially saying "It's not you, it's me." You'll almost always be offered a severance package, and sometimes even job placement assistance. Some firms will actually give you a head start and offer you a set period of time to actively search for another position while still on their payroll. They know it's harder for you to get a position if you don't have a job, so they are willing to spend a bit more on you to assist your transition. They have no obligation to do this. Unlike layoffs in a manufacturing environment, you shouldn't expect to be called back to the firm once conditions improve.

If you are fired for cause it may be because the firm has lost confidence in your abilities, or because you did something wrong. If your performance is simply poor but you tried your best, you are likely to be fired for cause but treated with respect and possibly offered severance. If you are fired for something really bad, like lying, stealing, or harassment, your firm may dismiss you quickly for cause and you may not get a severance package.

You shouldn't be surprised in any scenario. If a firm is well managed no one should be surprised with any personnel actions because the expectations were clear. Well run law firms constantly measure and evaluate performance. If your performance is not meeting the expectations of your firm you may land in hot water. If you are at a good firm, you may be given an opportunity to fix the issues. If your firm calls you in to discuss issues with your performance, you need to be humble and listen to their concerns. The worst thing you can do is to get defensive. You may be asked questions, or they may simply lay the issues on the table and tell you what needs to happen for you to restore their confidence.

Are there warning signs that you might be at risk of termination? Yes. Good firms communicate with their employees and ensure that everyone knows what's required. At other firms there may not be a great process and the risks are less clear. A performance improvement plan is not offered to everyone. To protect yourself in either situation, start by paying attention to your own performance metrics. If you are supposed to bill 150 hours every month and you only bill 100, eventually you are going to pay the price. You don't need to wait for a memo in that scenario. Regardless of the reasons behind your numbers, you shouldn't expect your firm to allow you to hang around forever if you can't meet the minimum productivity requirements.

Even if you are hitting your numbers, people may be dissatisfied with the quality of your work. If Partners who used to give you work no longer give you anything, there could be an issue. If those same Partners suddenly avoid any discussions with you and give you the cold shoulder, there probably is a problem. Not all Partners are good at providing feedback, so many will simply stop using you rather than invest their time into trying to coach you. In addition to the cold shoulder from some of the Partners, you may notice changes in how others interact with you. HR personnel or staff closely connected to firm leaders may suddenly seem more formal or distant. If the firm has decided to terminate you, several people in administration will know about the decision before you will. It may take days or even weeks to actually schedule the date to let you go, so some people at your firm may have to carry that knowledge, which can make their normal interactions with you stilted and uncomfortable. It's another reason why you should try to meet everyone. If you don't interact with many people you may miss big perceptual changes that are unfolding.

If you do find yourself in a termination situation don't panic. You should be dealt with professionally. You will usually be informed in a meeting in a discreet office or conference room. There will usually be at least 2 firm representatives in attendance. They want a witness in these meetings. It will be a short meeting. They won't argue the merits of the decision or entertain your rebuttal. They are there to deliver the decision. Even if your firm is generally adept at HR issues it doesn't mean that your immediate supervisor has experience firing people, so the meeting may be exceptionally awkward. Some firms have strict policies on how to handle terminations, so they may have no choice in how they handle your exit. You may be followed back to your office to pack your belongings. Your network and security access will have been cut by the time you get back to your desk. Don't take it personally. Some firms have similar procedures for people who voluntarily resign.

At the end of it all you may be offered a severance package. To receive any additional pay or benefits, a terminated employee almost always has to sign a release which documents the mutual agreement of the terms of your separation. Don't take the offer as an indicator that management has done something wrong and needs the protection from that waiver. They want it, but they don't need it. If you are ever offered a severance package take the time to review it later in a calmer environment. Don't sign anything you've just been handed. If you want to try to negotiate better terms you certainly can try, but in most cases, people simply take what is offered.

Being fired is a difficult thing to come to terms with, but always try to take the high road. Leave the firm with your dignity and let them talk later about how professional and classy you were on the way out. You may be able to retain good connections with the firm. Be professional and you will get through it. The vast majority of people who have been fired eventually find peace with the situation. Most people will find another position which they are better suited for and they end up happier as a result.

22
Your Secret Plan isn't Secret

Even if you love your current firm and you're doing well, your long term plans make take you in another direction. I've chatted with a lot of Associates over the years who enter private practice with a secret agenda. They aren't planning to become an Equity Partner. It's actually not much of a secret. Associates who can't envision themselves as a Partner someday often formulate a Plan B for their career. Their future plans usually fall into one of the following categories:

- Work in private practice for a few years, then jump to an in-house position
- Work BigLaw for a few years to make a lot of money, then downshift later to a smaller firm for more life balance
- Work in law for a few years, then pivot to the business world in a non-legal position
- Work as an attorney for a few years, then move to a legal admin position

These are very common themes which come up in conversations with mid-level attorneys. The topic gets more attention as Associates get closer to their seventh year of private practice. In fact, the subject occurs with such unfailing frequency with senior Associates, I am actually a bit surprised when the possibility doesn't get mentioned.

As a new Associate, you'll eventually meet other Associates who are several years ahead of you and they may be considering a transition to an in-house position. They are considering leaving private practice to go in-house, which means they'll practice law in a private or public company's legal department rather than a law firm. As a lawyer you will meet and possibly work with in-house or corporate General Counsels and on first look, it appears they have a pretty good deal.

While the actual details and requirements of these positions vary from company to company, it's not hard to see the appeal. Several years into practice many unsatisfied lawyers start to worry about a lifetime of misery. Their first few years were tough, and they imagine that the rest of their career will require the same level of effort and sacrifice. Whether you leave law firm life or not, odds are this option will cross your mind someday as well. Why is this such an attractive option? Some explore opportunities outside of private practice because they are concerned about not making Partner. Others simply want a different work-life balance. Sometimes they'll leave a firm to work for one of the firm's clients, maintaining a strong relationship with their former bosses.

Going in-house is a concept that some people mull over as a fantasy. It gives them comfort when times are tough. There are plenty of options out there, so the idea can easily turn into a reality with the right awareness of opportunities and connections. A move like this is completely legitimate and can be a great decision for those who make the leap out of private practice. But, like all things, there can be problems, so it is wise to look before you leap.

There are clearly some positive aspects that lure people to this option. In-house lawyers don't have to hunt down their next project. They don't track billable time like their colleagues in private practice. They have no requirements to develop clients. Often there is a more predictable working schedule.

Job security, job satisfaction, and work-life balance are 3 of the biggest drivers. You may find other positive aspects if you work in house, especially if you work for a larger corporation. These options are particularly appealing to young lawyers who want to spend more time with family. Positions at larger companies, government agencies, and even non-profits can offer more career predictability. If you are passionate about an issue you may find a position related to your specific interests. For example, if you are motivated by civil rights, there are many non-profits in this area and you may be able to work under their banner. There are also positions with governmental agencies.

The bigger the company, the more opportunities there may be. If you land an in-house job at a company like The Walt Disney Company, life will be somewhat more predictable than it can be in private practice. You aren't going to have to worry as much about losing your job due to an economic downturn because Disney isn't going away. You'll have a stable work environment with steps for promotion over the years. You'll have good benefits and your paychecks aren't ever going to bounce. You'll probably have a set amount of vacation every year and you'll take the time without fear. You'll know what to expect.

In a larger corporate environment, your first step transitioning to in-house may not be as the top General Counsel. You may begin as a junior member of the team. Some start with the title of Assistant General Counsel or Vice President. The experiential threshold for these positions can be surprisingly low. Sometimes three or four years is all that is required. Generally speaking, the lower the bar on the experience required, the lower the starting rung on the ladder and the lower the pay. Some of these positions cover a full spectrum of legal and business issues, so you may be used simply as a corporate generalist. Other positions, often in larger departments, are very specific. A position may deal strictly with one area, such as intellectual property or employment contracts. These opportunities can help you develop a specialization.

There are lawyers who go into private practice with the intention to simply work a few years in a law firm before they go in-house. It's a very common approach. A few years at a good law firm is great training and if you are lucky you will make contacts and even friends at your firm's clients. You may hear about opportunities directly from those contacts. If you want to go in-house you should plan for that pivot early in your career. Start to align yourself early to opportunities. Develop contacts and knowledge about the industry where you would like to work. If you want to be in-house at an energy company, you are going to have a lot more luck in landing that position if you have experience and contacts in the sector. As you develop as a lawyer you will have many opportunities to attend mandatory CLE, so try to look for topics that add to your knowledge in a specific area. Your local Bar Association may have a subgroup for that industry — if so, join the section.

One of the best resources is the Association of Corporate Counsel. This is a large professional association of in-house lawyers. The group has more than 35,000 members around the globe who represent more than 10,000 companies. It's a tremendous resource for networking, education, and advocacy. There are chapters around the country. If you are working in-house your company may pay for your annual membership. This group also has an excellent job board.

There are downsides to going in-house. At many in-house positions the pay is much lower than the pay for similar levels of experience at bigger law firms. If you have been adjusting your lifestyle over the years as your pay increased, it might be hard to take the pay cut or to manage smaller annual increases. Once you land an in-house position you probably won't be getting the lucrative productivity bonuses you received in private practice. You may also have limited growth opportunities. The money issue is pertinent on any pivot scenario. Workload requirements also vary. Some in house lawyers work just as hard as a GC as they did in private practice. Every company is different so don't expect every situation to be similar.

Some in-house legal departments are very small because they outsource most of their legal work. If you are in an environment like that, your options for promotion may be few and far between. You may also end up doing the same type of work often, so you'll have to be comfortable with that to do well.

If you work in a large law firm you may dream of moving to the slower pace of a smaller law office. If you are at a national or international firm, you may be compensated at the top of the local market's scale. That makes moving to a smaller firm a challenge, especially if you don't have your own clients. While smaller firms love hiring lawyers with big firm credentials they may be suspicious of your willingness to take a pay cut if it is significant.

Work-life balance is an issue many lawyers struggle with their entire career. Moving from a large law firm to a small one may create more free time in your schedule, or it may not. It entirely depends on the firm. There are some smaller firms which operate as sweat shops, so don't make a move without fully understanding the expectations of other firms you may be considering.

Transitioning to a non-billable role within your firm is an option for lawyers, but these are less common than in-house positions. At larger firms it is not uncommon to find JDs serving as Recruiting Directors or in other top firm management positions like Executive Directors or COOs. Most of these folks do not practice law in their positions. If you step into a non-billing position and stay there for several years, it may be hard to reenter the workforce later as a billing attorney.

If you are worried about your future prospects in private practice, speak with your mentor or section head at your firm. Often there are resources and solutions which can help you through any rough patch. Your goals in private practice may be easier to obtain than you realize. If you do make the decision to move, take your time and consider every aspect before you make any commitment.

23

When it's Time to Pack Your Bags

You hope that your firm will stand the test of time, but not all law firms live forever. I'll end my discussion with a visit to the law firm graveyard. Before I go there, it's extremely helpful to know how to identify some of the signals which may indicate that your firm is about to tank. What surprises some people is how quickly a firm can fall apart. The speed with which an established firm can unravel can be head spinning. There are some warning signs that can indicate the potential for troubles ahead. Many of the signs are universal, regardless of the size of the firm.

There is an important thing to consider here. Although law firms do die, for the most part their lawyers do not. Very few lawyers go down with the ship. They simply move on to another firm, often in small groups. How easily that transition occurs can depend on how well prepared you are for the situation. If you think your firm is going to fall apart you need an escape plan. As events unfold you may be thrown a lifeline. The worst thing that can happen is for you to pass up a good offer at another firm only to hear later that your current job is no longer secure at your dying firm.

Don't expect to receive official warning that things are falling apart. You are unlikely to receive a poor health report on your firm. Much of what occurs at a struggling law firm may never reach your desk. As an Associate your firm is unlikely to share information with you about growing problems they are facing, especially if the information is particularly troubling. You'll hear a lot of rumors. Most of what you do hear through official channels will be sanitized. During tough times your firm can't afford to lose people, so they are unlikely to share information which might encourage you to seek employment at a safer firm.

If there appears to be confirmation of troubles, don't panic. Watch your firm leadership in these scenarios. Confident leadership will confront issues head-on and offer honest assessments of what is going on at the appropriate time. The situation may be temporary. If your firm management isn't the best, you may see some signs of weakness. Are you noticing more closed-door meetings? Are there raised voices in those meetings? Is the firm trying to downplay recent departures with explanations and stories that don't add up? Has recruiting stopped? Do strong employees suddenly disappear? Is communication getting worse? Are you losing access to some information that you used to get? All of these can be signs that something bad is brewing. Keep your eyes open because there may soon be strong indicators of bigger problems ahead.

The biggest threat occurs when Partners leave. Every firm relies on its top performing Partners and when the best of them leave things can be quite difficult for those they leave behind. Partners quit their firms when they disagree with the firm's decisions. These are almost always decisions which impact compensation. Watch departing Partners because if enough people leave, it will kill a firm. Successful Partners are successful rainmakers. Some firms have a strong reliance on a small group of rainmakers and their departure can be very troubling. When a lawyer who consistently brings in new business leaves you must wonder about who will replace their success. Who is going to bring in the next big piece of work to feed everyone?

Departures also increase the potential for a negative morale impact. Senior lawyers are often part of the foundation of a firm. In addition to the loss of revenue, when they leave it can send a negative signal to the rest of the firm and the marketplace. The departure of several top people at once will get the attention of other law firms and recruiters, who will view the loss as blood in the water. If there is a succession of departures, an external narrative will form casting doubt on the viability of the firm.

Issues can also occur if a large client of the firm experiences trouble. It's smart to be knowledgeable about your customers. If you get a lot of work from a few clients, you should set up a Google alert to be notified of major news stories as they occur. This may help you stay on top of developments and opportunities and can help warn you if something bad is about to happen.

If you start hearing rumors about money problems at your own firm, pay more attention. Watch for changes in how money is spent. Cash is the life blood of any business. One of the most devastating occurrences that can happen is the cash call we mentioned earlier. This situation means that the firm lacks liquidity. A firm's value may be held up in accounts receivable — but that doesn't matter because the need for cash is immediate. Firms can survive a cash call, although it will really anger some Equity Partners.

Law firms always try to be diligent on expenses. Senior management spends a great deal of time developing their firm's budget each year. With so much planning involved, and a budget which requires approval at the highest level, there is an expectation that expenses will be predictable. Firms who find themselves with an unexpected loss of revenue or higher than expected expenses can be clumsy and reactionary as they struggle to preserve cash. If your firm is hoarding cash, they will shut off all non-essential payments. You may start to hear from vendors inquiring about delayed payments. Tensions will rise if your firm is not sure that it can afford payroll every other week.

Cash preservation mode is dangerous because the people at the top who are making the decisions in the crisis phase are not typically the ones with the best understanding of the various aspects of the firm's daily operations or expenses. One firm under considerable financial pressure decided to slow pay all their vendors, seeing this as a viable way to preserve their cash. Unfortunately, they didn't specify limits, so even the smallest charges went unpaid. Vendors quickly reacted and changed their payment terms. Some required payment up front. It's difficult to convince your nervous employees that everything is going to be okay when their everyday experience is showing something entirely different. If a courier won't take your documents to the courthouse without a ten dollar payment up front, something is clearly wrong.

When things get really tough layoffs are a common approach to reduce expenses, but they too often produce mixed results. While discharging unproductive employees may make sense, doing so in a large group spooks everyone else. Even targeted layoffs can raise concerns. For example, laying off the person who makes the coffee in the office probably doesn't save the firm much money. It does however force lawyers to make their own coffee rather than focus on their practice. And do you know what they are doing as they make their own coffee? They are standing around complaining to other lawyers about the situation, chipping away at morale and confidence in firm leadership.

Often the best and brightest Associates and staff see a layoff merely as the first bump against an iceberg. Fearing the entire ship will sink, they immediately connect with their networks and find a lifeline. The result can be undesired turnover, which can actually reduce revenue further, create morale problems, reduce productivity, and increase other costs. Layoffs can scare away a firm's best people — the very ones they were trying to protect.

Few firms own their offices, so they must pay expensive rents. Traditionally, larger law firms spend a great deal of money on class A office space in the most expensive parts of a city's central business district. Most significant office leases are at least 5 years in duration. The longer the term of commitment, the better the rates are. It's not uncommon for law firms to sign leaseholds for as long as 10 years. Some firms can find themselves with more office capacity than needed so they may sublease space. This is an admission of sorts that the office with a sublease has stopped growing. It may or may not be problematic. A much larger concern is when there seems to be hesitation to renew a lease. Partners who are in it for the long haul have little hesitation when it comes to signing a lease. Partners who are not committed to a longer term with the firm generally try to avoid long term liabilities. There is a message in leasehold decisions. If your lease expires in 9 months and you haven't heard a single word about a renewal or a move, it might be time to worry.

If you find another position and resign be mindful of how you submit your resignation and to whom. Offer a written resignation with a brief thank you and a timeline for your proposed last day, usually at least two weeks out. Don't offer any critiques of your current firm and do whatever you can to preserve your relationships. When you leave your firm, your goal is to be remembered as an honored alumnus. Your firm may accept your decision professionally or they may act as if they are bitterly scorned. It all depends on the level of professionalism and training at the firm. Regardless of their reaction, stick to your plan and be respectful and professional. Always take the high road.

24

Warnings from the Law Firm Graveyard

Much can be learned from the failure of previously successful firms. Some of the greatest firms that once existed are gone and their legacies now exist merely as residual or "remnant" assets owned by collection firms. Overconfidence, complacency, and inaction have hastened the demise of many firms. While there are numerous factors in any failed business, ultimately the buck stops somewhere. Firm management can either safely guide a firm through difficult times or drive it straight into bankruptcy.

All businesses will experience challenges. While many larger law firms maintain significant cash reserves, not every firm keeps sufficient dry powder to help them survive hard times. In fact, many law firms, especially smaller ones, distribute much of their cash in year-end profit distributions to satisfy their equity group, leaving empty coffers and a slimmer margin of error if things don't go as planned. Well managed firms understand that every decade in the last century has had a recession (2 consecutive quarters of economic decline). External factors are an issue for all firms, so the nature of the business should not be a surprise to anyone. The real lessons lie in how firms respond, manage their resources, and the expectations of their own people during difficult times. When you examine failed firms, you will see clear examples of poor decisions by management. Often the harm does not come from a particular decision; it comes from inaction and the lack of a timely response to a rising issue. A single event can cause a chain reaction of damaging consequences. Good firm leaders are proactive and engaged, and nurture open lines of communication with the attorneys and staff. They are the voice of the firm and when something bad happens everyone looks to them for direction. Poor leaders merely react, often engaging only after a problem has occurred.

In a disaster scenario the worst thing possible is for management to hide behind closed doors. Some firm leaders view the industry from behind the complacency of their own walls. They measure everything by what makes sense in their closed world. They don't take broader external factors into consideration and they underestimate the risks. They don't truly understand the motivation of their people. They may think their kingdom is surrounded by a bountiful forest, but only because they aren't paying attention to drought conditions. This is why so many leaders are caught unprepared when the wildfire races through their firm. In failure scenarios, firm leadership teams are unable to control the issues, their people flee, and the firm ultimately dies.

Burelson LLP (2005–2015): Diversification is important
Burelson LLP is a great example of the risks of putting all your eggs into one basket. This law firm focused primarily on clients engaged in oil and gas production. At its high water mark it boasted more than 140 lawyers. Life was good for the firm as the price of oil soared. Then it fell.

Burleson had attracted strong talent and the firm expanded into active energy regions across the country. As the fortunes of oil companies faded, so did their expenditures on legal services. Hit by a one-two punch, the firm lost several key Partners to their competitors at a time when the price of oil was falling rapidly.

Burleson could not sustain itself and shut its doors at the end of 2015. The price of oil eventually rebounded and the demand for energy law recovered. Unfortunately, Burleson, like many other firms, did not have the cash reserves to sustain themselves through a long slowdown.

Jenkins & Gilchrest (1951–2007): Profit over common sense

Jenkins and Gilchrest was a flagship Dallas law firm. From their founding in 1951 the firm had recorded great success and grew into a national practice with more than 600 lawyers by the time they ran into trouble. At the start of 1998 the firm had only 325 lawyers. By the end of the year the firm had grown to over 400. They launched an ambitious Chicago office which was managed by a prominent tax attorney. The firm made a fortune promoting the Chicago office's tax planning practice. Unfortunately, their tax schemes were problematic and by following their advice, their clients cheated the government out of millions in tax revenue. In 2003 the government laid charges against the tax Partners, including conspiracy to defraud the IRS, tax evasion, and impeding and impairing the lawful functioning of the IRS. The firm parted ways with the attorneys involved but was still on the hook for their actions.

They could not shake the damage to their reputation. It's hard to recruit new Partners when your firm is viewed as promoting tax evasion. Equity Partners began to flee. One group of bad actors brought down the entire firm. After considerable negotiation, the firm admitted wrongdoing, paid a 76 million dollar penalty and folded their tent. Some people went to prison. The remaining lawyers were scooped up by other firms around the country.

Howrey (1956–2011): Be careful in merger talks

Once a merger talk becomes public the marketplace is immediately filled with assumptions. The market often assumes the smaller Partner of a merger is agreeable to being acquired because of some weakness. There doesn't have to be any merit to the argument, but the basic assumption is that a firm wouldn't sell out unless it had to. Walking away from merger talks can seriously damage a firm's brand. Even if the smaller firm has very legitimate reasons not to accept an offer, some may view the smaller firm as being "left at the altar" because of some terrible circumstance.

Howrey was a successful firm that encountered some trouble as several high-profile attorneys left for other opportunities. Firm revenues slipped, and PPP reportedly dropped below $900,000, which was a substantial fall for the firm. Fearing that their success might be eroding, they began talks with other high flying firms. Winston & Strawn and Howrey discussed combining, but ultimately there were some serious client conflict issues that killed the possibility. Not everyone at the firm was happy to see the talks end. Rather than walk away empty handed, Winston attracted several key attorneys from Howrey soon after the talks concluded, snagging profitable clients in the process. With the situation worsening and with few prospects for recovery, Howrey threw in the towel and closed their doors.

Brobeck, Phleger & Harrison (1926–2003): Panic kills

Brobeck was a California based firm which learned the hard way that hot practice areas aren't always sustainable. The firm had more than 1,000 attorneys and staff and represented many technology companies. The firm put a great deal of faith in the continued success of their technology clients, so much so they reportedly took equity in tech start-ups in lieu of payment. This might have seemed brilliant in the dot-com era, but eventually many of the early internet startups burned through their cash. Brobeck rode the crest of the wave during the boom of the dot-com era. They crashed on the sea floor when the bottom fell out of the tech sector. Some of their most profitable clients failed. The recession of 2001 sealed their fate. With revenue slipping, the firm was forced to borrow money to fund Partner compensation obligations. Rumors circulated about the firm locking people out of their retirement accounts, causing some to panic. Firm management restructured a growing debt load and tried in vain to find a merger Partner. They engaged in merger talks with Morgan Lewis, but the talks failed. Weeks later, about 150 Brobeck lawyers jumped ship and joined Morgan Lewis. Brobeck had no choice but to liquidate.

Thelen (1924–2009): Credit can be a life saver, or not

Thelen was another California success story that had been around since the Roaring Twenties. The firm had been growing for years through acquisitions and reached a new level of prominence after a merger with Brown Raysman in late 2006. Problems with the combination were reported almost immediately. While many felt the cultural differences between the firms would smooth themselves out, the equity compensation systems proved to be much more difficult to amalgamate. Partners are generally patient and willing to give new systems a chance, but many began to wonder aloud if the merger had been a terrible mistake. The firm suffered some high-level defections and decided to seek safe ground through another merger but couldn't find a suitable partner.

Partners began to leave, exposing a fatal mistake with the firm's credit facilities. The primary lender had issued credit with a covenant that restricted the number of Partners who could depart within a 12 month period. Essentially, if a certain number of Partners left, the bank could cut them off — and they did. Firms which cannot afford payroll don't last long. In fact, the one thing a firm needs to survive when Partners depart is access to additional credit. With busted covenants and no liquidity, the banks shut down their credit facilities and the speed of Partner departures increased. By the end of 2008 they drew up plans to shutter the firm.

Dewey & LeBoeuf (1909–2012): Don't cook the books

Dewey was another high-flying firm, boasting more than 1,000 lawyers with a dozen offices serving top clients. The firm had very impressive Partners, some of whom were secured with lucrative guarantees. As with other larger firms, they had developed a tremendously expensive infrastructure which relied on continued growth to be sustained.

The recession in 2008 had an enormous impact and led to a major slowdown of work from their corporate clients. Unable to scale down expenses, the firm tried desperately to portray itself in a better light, fearing any bad news would hamper their recruiting efforts. Not all their efforts were legit, and it was alleged that they were falsifying some of the numbers. The firm made fraudulent modifications to financial statements to satisfy the lending covenants they made with several banks. They were soon tripped up by their own book cooking. Their creditors sounded alarm bells and suddenly everyone was aware of their precarious situation. The firm tried to take corrective action. Financials were restated.

Partners began to look at other options as the situation worsened. They tried to save cash by cancelling their summer Associate program, which merely highlighted their financial woes. Ugly conflicts in the firm's leadership became public knowledge and some shocking comments on email were leaked to the media. The firm published a WARN notice, a federal regulation which requires larger companies to give at least 60 days of advance notice of mass layoffs. With its foundation crumbling, the firm didn't survive long enough to complete the warning period. Partners scattered to other firms and the doors were shut. Due to the financial fraud, lawsuits haunted the firm's principals and managers for years to follow.

Arter Hadden (1843–2003: No one lives forever

Arter Hadden's byline was once: "Solutions for business today and tomorrow." Past performance is not, however, an indicator of future performance, even if a firm is 160 years old. The firm launched before the American Civil War and had survived countless economic storms. In the 1980s and 1990s the firm began an aggressive expansion push across the country, acquiring smaller firms as it moved west from its home base in Ohio. Convinced of their growth trajectory, they took on expensive leases and built an impressive infrastructure throughout the 1990s. Unfortunately, their success attracted poachers who began to pick off some of their talented Partners. They weren't able to react fast enough, and soon found themselves with more space than people in some markets. Empty floors became huge liabilities. Dark hallways are never a good situation for recruiting and retention. With high overhead and declining revenue, their struggle soon became public and the rest of the marketplace pounced. Partners were poached, and the firm had no choice but to surrender and close their doors.

25

Some Final Tips

Over the years I've seen various trends with successful lawyers. You can enhance your odds by adopting some good habits like they did, at the start of your career.

Time entry matters: One of the best things you can do on day one is get into the habit of recording your billable time daily. Don't go home until all your time is recorded into the system. I can't stress this one enough. If you fail to master this, it will haunt you for the rest of your career. Don't like time entry? Too bad, it's not going away. It's part of the job. It's the part of the job that gets your firm paid. Many lawyers hold their time and try to enter it weekly or, god forbid, monthly. If you aren't entering your time daily I promise you, you will cheat yourself out of the credit you deserve. You will make mistakes if you rely on your memory from days or weeks ago. Your clients may comb through the bills they receive with a fine tooth comb. Some use outside services to audit your bills. You simply cannot afford to have errors. Since time entry is the starting point of all revenue, your firm is watching you.

When given work take a moment to confirm the work requirements first. This may be easier said than done because some work will simply be dropped on you. If possible, when a Partner gives you an assignment, ask three questions:

- When is the project due? You can't miss deadlines. You will often be given a shorter timeline than the client requested because the Partner needs time to review your work.

- How much time should you put into the project? You could spend the rest of your life researching an issue. Ask up front about an acceptable amount of time to invest and you will reduce the risk of them writing off time that they feel is extraneous.

- What is the billing number? You need to record that time to get credit for it. If they don't have a number yet (for a new client) get a provisional number so you can record something.

Asking these questions will save you major headaches.

Be Careful with Email: For starters, be mindful of the Reply All option. Many great attorneys have embarrassed themselves by inadvertently broadcasting a reply to a message to the entire firm. More damaging is when you accidently send an email to the wrong recipient. A fatal mistake can occur if you send sensitive information to the wrong recipient. I've seen careers ruined by careless messaging. Emails live forever. Even if you delete them they still exist on a server somewhere at your firm. Don't write anything that you would be embarrassed about if it were read out loud at a meeting. Also write emails with the assumption that someone is going to forward them to other people, even the ones with sensitive information. If you write something horrible in an email someone may print it or save it. It could come back on you years from now. Don't forget that many lawyers give their staff full access to their email, so whatever you write to them is being read by the staff as well.

Connect to the industry: Start connecting to other professionals as soon as you can. There are many legal associations and subgroups you can join. While in school you should check out the American Bar Association and join as a student member. There is literally no good reason not to join. Get on their mailing list and you will receive a continuous flow of relevant information. You can access their research, attend their meetings, even take a student leadership role in the organization. Once you start your first job keep looking for other groups to join. You can learn a lot more about the various practice groups in the industry and start to think about your future specialization. You will also find many legal publications that offer a non-stop stream of information on cases, issues, trends, and more, all relevant to the legal profession. It's wise to spend a few minutes in the morning looking over the industry's headlines.

Meet everyone: During your orientation you will likely meet a lot of people. You probably won't remember all the names and if you work in a large firm you may not see some of the people you meet again for some time. Many of the busier people at the firm may not have time to meet you at a welcome breakfast. They may be on a client call if the HR team walks you around the office for your initial tour. When you start get a copy of the firm's organizational chart and start highlighting all the people you meet. Make it a goal to meet everyone on the list. At least once a month try to walk the halls and introduce yourself to anyone you don't know. This will go a long way into creating relationships with your coworkers and will put you on the radar for other Partners. While many people will seem too busy to chat, most people really appreciate someone going out of their way to introduce themselves. If you aren't on LinkedIn yet sign up and put some time into it. It's free and it is currently the number one hunting destination for recruiters because of its ease of use.

Don't eat at your desk every day: Along the lines of the point above, once you get really busy it will become easy to eat lunch at your desk. A lot of people do it. It's an easy way to catch up during some quiet time. You can shut your office door, read the news headlines, check your social media, powernap, whatever. It's probably the one time of the day where someone won't be looking for you. While this is not frowned upon, there are many reasons why you shouldn't spend lunch alone. If you are an introvert at least try to dine with others at least once a week. Each week gives you five excellent opportunities to connect with people. Odds are you will find groups of people who like each other and frequently eat together. Go with them if you can. Over lunch you will learn more about the lives of the people you work with. Get out, get to know people, make friends, and grow your connections.

Break the 9 to 5 routine: Odds are you'll settle into a routine for your office hours. You'll end up setting your working hours around things like your domestic routines, your commute, etc. I have been the first guy and the last guy in the office. Some Partners like to start work before the sun rises. Some get a later start and get energized after lunch. Many will pick a weekend to come in and get caught up. Lawyers who work outside of the standard office hours often cite their desire to get in a few hours without the normal distractions of client calls, admin issues, and the general traffic of daily office life. Even if you find the ideal schedule it's wise to occasionally mix it up a bit to encounter folks with different schedules. Come in earlier at times and occasionally stay late. There is a very different vibe between the people who are at the office at 6 a.m. on Monday and those who are hanging out at 6 p.m. on Friday. Remember, your goals to meet as many people as possible. Casting a wider net will create more opportunities. At one firm a group of Partners met on Fridays just as everyone else was leaving for the weekend. These Partners preferred to let the traffic die down before they left for the day. Eventually, they found each other and developed a routine where they would all gather for a quick drink and talk about the events of the week. Eventually others joined them, realizing that an informal clique was forming, and friendships were being made. Better yet, this casual down time actually created a forum for discussions which led to highly productive cross selling opportunities.

Don't take undue advantage of flexible work schedules: Not yet anyway — not at the start of your career. "Face time "is a concept that essentially means that some people place more value on employees who are in the office than those who are not. While it is entirely possible to do much of your work remotely it's unwise to do so at the start of your career. Mentoring and business relationships are vastly enhanced when there is personal, one-on-one communication. If your relationship is mostly via email you aren't going to get the usual questions from a Partner about your weekend plans, your hobbies, your kid's soccer practice, etc. It's all these little things that help create stronger connections. If your office or workspace is always dark, people may not think you are available to work, or worse yet, it may create a perception that you aren't hard working. It's also evident that older attorneys who spent a significant portion of their youth in the office expect to see their Associates in the office as well. It's not uncommon for a Partner to walk the hallways seeking help on a big assignment. The pop in visit can produce work opportunities. Out of sight is often out of mind. Frequent time away from the office may produce the worst question of all in the hallways, when a Partner walks by and asks if you still work there.

Try to make a difference in the lives around you: There are a thousand little things you can do to make a difference at your firm. Many of these actions take only a moment. Think of the old random acts of kindness concept and look for a simple thing. If you work at a larger firm, odds are at any given time someone in the firm is dealing with a personal challenge. Someone is dealing with medical issues, family issues, or some crisis which is making their life stressful — and often there is no outward sign of the issues. Realize that many people working for you will not bring their personal struggles to your attention because they don't want to imposition you. Invest in people around you and you'll find them there for you in your moments of need.

Be the hero: During the early days of your practice you will have many opportunities to come to the rescue when a busy Partner needs additional help. Often these small projects will not produce a lasting workload, but they will help cement your reputation as a team player. It's one thing to have the support of the Partners you work with daily. It's entirely another thing to have the support of Partners in other sections. A Partner once complained to me that he couldn't get help on an urgent project one evening. It turned out that the Associates in his section where attending a happy hour that evening. The person who came back to work after the happy hour was viewed very positively and had expanded access to the partner after coming to the rescue.

Understand how recruiting works and don't get suckered: Once you are established in your career, especially at a large law firm, you will start to hear from recruiters. If you are good at what you do and you're working at a good firm, you may hear from recruiters every single day, and even possibly multiple times a day. Most of them will attempt to lure you to a land of milk and honey. While there are some awesome recruiters out there, you may also encounter some people who will tell you anything to get you to move. There are thousands of recruiters and many of them work on quotas. If they don't get enough candidates in their pipeline they could lose their job. To them it's a numbers game and you're simply one of the numbers. Odds are they called you and 20 other lawyers that day. The upside for them is great because recruiters typically charge up to 25% of your annual salary if they place you somewhere. It's a very difficult job but very lucrative. Placing a single junior attorney at a national law firm can easily earn the recruiter more than $50,000. When that much money is at stake you can see why they are motivated to convince you to make a career change. Your best interests might not be their number one motivator. That being said, the good recruiters are worth their weight in gold. Even some of the less than stellar recruiters can be helpful if they are connected to the right firm. Some firms have dozens of agencies on their approved vendor list, but the people who oversee hiring likely have a small, select group of trusted recruiters.

If you do engage a recruiter, follow their instructions. If they are submitting you to a firm, don't attempt direct contact with the firm without informing them because you may complicate the recruiting process. A recruiter who can help you get a better deal might be knocked out of the process with a firm if you contact that firm's HR directly before the terms are agreed upon. Most of the recruiting process is supposed to follow a specific process.

Be cautious and protect your reputation. It's never wrong to take a phone call but be careful when dealing with recruiters in public. Be seen having lunch with a well-known recruiter and word of the meeting might get back to your boss. You may not be aware that you are sending a signal, so be cautious. Be warned, not every recruiter is as discrete as they should be.

26
Final Thoughts

As you embark on your career you will be faced with a multitude of experiences, regardless of which firm or practice you decide to work in. Just like in all other careers, some days in legal will be a challenge, and some will be a joy. There will be days early on when you might question the path you are on. There will be days later when you will be thankful you're where you are.

Don't give up. Too many young lawyers get a bad start with their first job and then assume their entire career will be a disaster. There will be things that are beyond your control. Never forget that every problem has a solution. If you continue moving forward many rewards await you. There are so many great things ahead if you stick with your plan. You may meet some of the best friends you will ever have. You will work with brilliant, inspirational people. You will develop expertise and be well-regarded by your peers. With an open mind and a willingness to learn and work hard, you can become an amazing lawyer.

Your efforts can allow you to reach heights you never imagined. You can make a great living and become financially secure. This success can allow you to accomplish wonderful things for yourself, your family, your community, and your profession. To be truly great, you should pass those skills and your wisdom down to others who follow your path.

Enjoy your career.

Made in the USA
Columbia, SC
24 December 2018